WORK SMART

WORK SMART

USE YOUR BRAIN AND BEHAVIOR
TO MASTER THE FUTURE OF WORK

JENNIE BYRNE, MD, PHD

NEW DEGREE PRESS

WORK SMART
Use Your Brain and Behavior to Master the Future of Work

ISBN	979-8-88504-445-5	*Paperback*
	979-8-88504-487-5	*Hardcover*
	979-8-88504-468-4	*Ebook*

Table of Contents

Introduction

———

Have you wondered why you can recognize someone's face before remembering their name or how you know them?

It turns out there are individual cells in our brains, called neurons, specifically attuned to recognizing faces. I first learned of these neurons in the summer of 1995, when I was a new college grad and eager to start working. I did a gap year while I took my MCATs and applied to MD and PhD programs. I had a job planned for a research assistant position in New Haven, Connecticut, where I would work in a lab that looked at cells in the brains of monkeys that coded for facial recognition.

Surprise—there were individual neurons in the monkey brain which coded for monkey faces. The hardwiring of our brains includes attention to faces. Who knew? Unfortunately, the assistant in the position decided to stay at the last minute, so I ended up working in a lab that looked at the startle response in Vietnam veterans. I was so disappointed not to see the face cells in the monkey brains firsthand.

Being a *neuroscience researcher*, I observe the world around me and think about how to navigate the world with my expertise in the human brain. Being a psychiatrist and a psychotherapist, I am in the business of changing human behavior through a variety of tools, including cognitive behavioral therapy and medications. As a *leader* and *executive*, I see firsthand the importance of what most people call EQ (emotional quotient or people skills): understanding how human beings work. I use these skills to help individuals and teams function better together to achieve organizational goals.

Monkeys are not the only ones who are fascinated by faces. Humans are powerfully attracted to looking at other human faces. Have you seen an image of human eye movements looking at a piece of art? The human eye will automatically spend most of the visual time looking at the faces in the painting. Moreover, we will scan back and forth between the faces of different people on the canvas, seeking a relationship between the people.

Think back to your last virtual meeting on Zoom or another videoconferencing platform. Did you notice you were fatigued after the call? Now envision all the things which were happening in your brain while you were looking at twenty different faces. Your facial neurons were firing like crazy, and your eyes were constantly scanning back and forth between the faces looking for relationships but finding none. This process exhausts and distresses your brain.

What about looking at your own image on Zoom? Have you noticed *you simply cannot stop looking at your own face*? Your brain creates this phenomenon. Most humans have great difficulty not looking at themselves in a mirror. In addition to facial recognition neurons, our brain has specific neurons designed to help us mirror others. So, when we look at our own face in the mirror, we activate both face and mirror cells.

Many of my colleagues tell me they want to return to the office because "I'm tired of looking at myself on Zoom." When I show them how to turn off their self-view and tell them to get rid of their face, they are surprised. "Oh, I can do that?" This feeling has a name—virtual meeting (VM) fatigue. A recent study (Ratan 2022) found 14.9 percent greater VM fatigue for women than men and 11.1 percent higher for Asian than for White participants. Facial dissatisfaction mediated the VM gender and race/ethnicity differences. The study suggests practical approaches to mitigating VM fatigue could be implementing tech features that reduce self-focused attention during VMs, like using avatars.

Recently, my friends, colleagues, and I discussed their plans for work. The majority of them discussed in person versus virtual. They were making decisions about when and how to return to the physical office versus keep doing Zoom. Most of the conversation concerned the obstacles they face in person or with Zoom and *how they longed to return to the old days* when things were simpler.

WERE THE OLD DAYS REALLY THE GOOD DAYS?

In the fall of 1998, I was an energetic and idealistic MD/PhD student in my lab (literally) knee-deep in wires and cables. I prepared a Skinner box (a device designed to measure behavior without any outside stimuli like noise or images) to do an experiment to understand how the brain paid attention. The occupant of the Skinner box was my *star* rat. I loved my star rat. He performed for me over and over again, without fail, no matter what pressures I subjected him to. I disliked my other rats, who were erratic, inconsistent, and doing things on their own schedule.

My star rat resembled the American *ideal worker* (Schulte 2022). Never late or tired, he showed up when I wanted, and he did what I wanted over and over and over again with surprising consistency. Of course, rats being rats, I didn't give much consideration to his home life in a sad little cage. He had no friends, no toys, and nothing to do but sit in his cage, waiting for me to take him out for another experiment. Maybe the rat preferred being on the job, working hard, and pleasing me.

People are more complicated than rats, but maybe the ideal worker has appealed for many years because we like to think of workers like rats. Regular, predictable, consistent, and reliable. And for some people, like my star rat, perhaps this works. Perhaps they don't want to do anything except work. The vast majority of people have other needs, like love, relationships, family, hobbies, and physical needs. Asking them to all be ideal workers who live in a lonely and boring cage, waiting for the chance to come to the office and work nonstop, is unrealistic. Thinking of my star rat and comparing it to the way most Americans feel like they need to show up for work makes me sad and angry. There has to be a better way.

WHY DO OUR CURRENT WAYS OF WORKING SUCK?

For many people, the future of work involves virtual work. For example, Upwork estimates that 22 percent of the workforce (36.2 million Americans) will work remotely by 2025 (Ozimek 2021).

Unfortunately, the current state of virtual work is far from ideal. Burnout is common. A survey by monster.com found that 69 percent of employees are experiencing burnout symptoms while working at home (Monster Staff 2020). Many virtual workers find themselves working longer hours. A study by Mental Health America (MHA) and Flexjobs found that 37 percent of surveyed remote workers report working more hours than while working in the office (Reynolds 2021).

As the stigma of mental health decreases, people are speaking out. In the same MHA study, more than 75 percent of all workers agree that workplace stress affects their mental health, leading to depression and anxiety, and 48 percent of workers say they lack emotional support at work to help them manage this daunting task (Reynolds 2021).

However, organizations are changing rapidly, and there are bright spots. The number of people choosing virtual work will increase. Companies that are successful at virtual work will also be successful at recruiting and retaining talent.

In a survey of 10,000 employees surveyed by the Becker Friedman Institute for Research in Economics at the University of Chicago, 30 percent of those respondents told researchers they were more productive and engaged working from home (Apollo Technical 2022). A Slack survey of

9,000 workers in six countries found that 72 percent prefer a hybrid remote-office model (Slack 2020). In this survey, only 12 percent preferred to always work in an office setting, and 13 percent preferred to always work from home.

Some of the tech tools we initially used for virtual work are not the panacea for virtual work. Growth has slowed—Zoom stock price rose, then returned to prepandemic price. Similarly, Microsoft Teams topped 270 million users in December 2021, then growth slowed.

Mastering work in the virtual space may be more important than many people think. Talent, especially in the millennial and GenZ groups, will likely require successful virtual work environments. A survey by Owl Labs found that 59 percent of respondents said they would be more likely to choose an employer who offered remote work compared to those who didn't (Apollo Technical 2022).

Virtual work may help counteract gender and race biases and assumptions from an in-person setting. However, it is important to understand what works from a human brain and behavior viewpoint.

Finally, the new era of virtual work may contribute to societal inequities. A Pew Research Center study in 2020 found a clear class divide among new teleworkers who can and cannot telework. For example, 56 percent of upper-income workers say they can mostly do their job from home. However, only 37 percent of middle-income and 24 percent of lower-income workers can work virtually. There are also racial disparities: 57 percent of Asian Americans can work from home, 39 percent of White, 37 percent of Black, and 29 percent of Hispanics (Parker 2021).

The stakes are higher than we think, and we need to quickly evolve how we understand virtual work.

WHAT CAN I DO NOW TO MAKE WORK NOT SUCK?

While some of the solutions to virtual work are likely to come from big ideas from creative individuals, we can implement small solutions now. Whether you are an entry-level employee, a manager, a leader, or a CEO, you can take action now to make virtual work easier and more enjoyable. I see most people waiting for someone else to give them the answers:

"Human resources (HR) will tell me how to work with people virtually."

"IT will tell me how to use my tech successfully."

"My boss will tell me how to manage my time working from home."

At the beginning of the pandemic, I was also waiting for the answers. I waited for organizational leaders to tell me how to work virtually from home. I waited for the media to publish amazing articles on how I could improve my performance working from home. After a few months, the answers were not coming quickly enough to help me. I decided to do my own research and try to connect the dots between my knowledge of the human brain, behavior, creativity, and how to work successfully in a virtual setting.

I have now, like many others, been working virtually for over two years at the time of this writing. I have found cognitive frameworks based on my experience, which have helped me make a series of small changes in my own work settings. Along the way, I found other people who are also looking for small steps they can take now to make their virtual workspace better for themselves and their teams.

The future is now, and despite the discomfort and pain, there is good reason for optimism. We have the opportunity to synthesize our knowledge about the history of work, and about our brains and our behavior, to inform how we work in the future. We have the opportunity to challenge old assumptions and work smarter. *The future of work is about being better humans.*

- Are you frustrated with working virtually with your teams?
- Were you frustrated by your in-person workplace prepandemic?
- Do you want to shake things up?

If your work has shifted to virtual/hybrid, or if you are considering new ways to work, you have an amazing opportunity today. You can make small, pragmatic changes that can greatly improve your work satisfaction. Making choices to work smarter today can improve both the short- and long-term performance and satisfaction of your team. You can learn how to infuse more humanism into your workplace and become a better human at work.

If you are like me, you have another fifteen-plus years of work ahead of you, and you don't want it to suck.

I encourage you to join me. Embrace the discomfort and try new answers because the future is now. Why go back to the old way of doing things when we have so many opportunities ahead? Let's disrupt this work paradigm together.

CHAPTER 1

Escape from Languishing

During the pandemic, did you:

- Feel time moving in strange ways?
- Experience a breakdown of boundaries between home and work?
- Miss out on a sense of play?
- Have difficulty finding meaning?

It turns out there is a term for these feelings: *languishing*. The good news is people can find ways to escape the status quo of languishing and find time for space and flow. Creativity is one way to promote flow states and improve your mood and brain functioning and includes creative problem-solving not related to creating art per se.

LANGUISHING IS THE NEW NORMAL

On August 17, 2020, I realized there was a new normal.

My family endured the first summer of the pandemic in fear, canceling all camps, activities, and vacations. We were eager for the school year to start, anticipating we would feel more *normal* with the school year routines. We were in for a rude awakening.

It was my kids' first day of school as an eighth grader and a sixth grader. They were attending virtual school in our unfinished lower level, the newly named *one-room school-room*. I sat in my home office, my husband sat at a living room desk, and summer was over. I stared at a small laptop screen, preparing to plow through hundreds of emails and a day of back-to-back Zoom meetings at work.

Over the next few months, time moved in strange directions. I expected the return to school to feel more normal, and time would fall into a neat pattern of school, work, and play. It didn't. Time seemed to move slowly during the workday, and I ran out of energy before I got to lunch. After school, the kids couldn't hang out with friends and couldn't do sports or other fun activities. They sat all afternoon alternating between homework, Instagram, and TikTok. I wasn't much better. Evenings dragged on with Netflix binges and not much else.

At other times, I felt so busy I didn't have a spare moment to myself. The back-to-back calls made me feel stuck to my chair, and getting up to go to the bathroom seemed like a luxury. The emails and DMs kept coming all day long, with endless pings on my monitors and phone. After work, there were more tasks. Going to the grocery store became a big production. We searched for toilet paper, came home, and wiped groceries down with Clorox.

There was a sense of drag, endless tasks, and not much in the way of play. It was like Jack Nicolson's character in *The Shining*: "All work and no play makes Jack a dull boy" (Kubrick 1980).

During the pandemic, people asked each other, "How are you doing?"

The other person often paused and answered, "Okay, I guess," or "Good, considering…" Typically, we attributed our feelings to things not going well, work felt wrong, home felt strange, accomplishments, holidays, events, everything felt on hold.

This feeling has a name—**languishing**.

Adam Grant is an organizational psychologist and a leading expert on how we can find motivation and meaning, rethink assumptions, and live more generous and creative lives. He is recognized as one of the world's ten most influential management thinkers and one of Fortune's 40 under 40.

Notably, Adam published his best-selling book *Think Again* in 2021. So, Adam should have been on top of the world during the pandemic, but was he? No. Ever the self-observer, Adam wrote a *New York Times* article on his own sense of languishing and struggles with creative flow during the pandemic. This piece went viral and was the most-read *New York*

Times article of 2021 (Staff of the Morning 2021) and the most-saved article across all platforms (Grant 2021).

In a *Happiness Labs* podcast (Santos 2022), Adam told the story of how he realized his pandemic feeling of *meh* wasn't depression or burnout but a different emotional state. Languishing is the absence of well-being. Once he put a name on it, things clicked, and he wanted to actively do something to get out of this languishing. He started playing *Mario Kart* online, which he enjoyed as a child.

What made *Mario Kart* important to escape his sense of languishing was twofold. First, while he played *Mario Kart,* he didn't check email, social media, or his phone. He reclaimed time confetti with larger blocks of uninterrupted time where he entered a flow state. Second, he found a way to connect with his family living in different places. He fondly recalls the sense of excitement he and his family felt when they woke up and prepared for a fun *Mario Kart* game.

Adam found meaning again in playing *Mario Kart* because he connected with his family and entered a flow state again. He believes *finding flow and meaning is a path out of a languishing state*, although the path to flow and meaning will be different for each individual.

When I think back to my experience in the fall of 2020, I see I was languishing. Happily, since then, I have found ways out of languishing by creating time and space for flow states.

FIND FLOW THROUGH PLAY

Languishing and flow are opposites, but they are also similar. Both languishing and flow have an other-world type of feeling, different from typical human mind-racing. Languishing is an unpleasant floating where you are present in the moment in a negative, disembodied type of place. Flow is a highly pleasurable state where time changes and you feel connected to the moment and what you are doing. Getting out of languishing means getting into flow, and *one of the best ways to access flow is through play.*

If you watch human children, puppies, baby bears, or other young mammals, you likely see them play. In the past ten years, brain and behavior researchers studied the neuroscience of play and its benefits (Siviy 2016). The conservation of play happens through evolution. Many animals play, particularly young mammals. Play is developmentally important, and studies have shown that if rats are deprived of play, they become socially, emotionally, and cognitively impaired.

Brain areas most likely involved in the modulation of play include regions within the prefrontal cortex, dorsal and ventral striatum, regions of the amygdala, and habenula. In other words, play engages not one but an entire network of brain areas, including both the older and newer parts of the brain.

At a neurochemical level, increased release of endogenous cannabinoids in the amygdala may serve to facilitate play. Endogenous cannabinoids are naturally occurring chemicals in the human body, similar to the chemicals found in marijuana and hemp. Interestingly, THC (but not CBD) may activate the same neuron receptors as play. If you support the use of legal marijuana, you could argue that taking external THC in the form of marijuana may help people enter play states more easily.

Play is a critical developmental activity in young mammals, which leads to adults who are better able to navigate an ever-changing social, emotional, and cognitive landscape. More recent research shows the importance of play for adults. In a 2021 article, Peter Gray, a research professor of psychology and neuroscience at Boston College who studies play for a living, said:

"Some of the many benefits of making time for playing include a reduction in stress and anxiety, increased social bonding, an instant mood boost, and a way to foster creativity and problem-solving" (Paier 2021).

Taking the advice of Adam Grant and Peter Gray, I carved small chunks of time out of my days to play. After creating the time, I tried new things—the sillier, the better. I tried learning the electric bass. I tried purple mascara. I tried online dance classes where the instructor wore fluorescent hot pants and cursed at me to improve my twerking.

In addition to play, another powerful way to decrease languishing is through creativity and creative problem-solving.

ESCAPE FROM THE STATUS QUO

During the fall of 2020, I had a realization. I focused on being "a professional" to get my team through the pandemic crisis. I did not play, and I did no creative work. On one work call, we made small talk, and someone asked what we studied in college. I shared with the group that I started college as a music performance major on the bassoon. People were surprised and curious to learn more. I realized I didn't share the creative side of myself at work. Why? I felt like it was not good enough or big enough to celebrate. I felt it would hurt my professional reputation. These ideas started early for me, even in childhood.

My aunt Bobbie was a magical figure for me growing up. My grandfather, Sol, died when I was four years old (of note, he was the only other physician in my family). Aunt Bobbie was his little sister and a close friend of my grandmother. Aunt Bobbie was all the things my immediate family was not. She lived alone in a small house outside of Philadelphia, and when we would visit her, the first thing which greeted us was a hallway filled with a collage of family photos dating back from the 1800s to the present day.

Walking into her house was like walking through a funky and tidy design lab. Her artwork was everywhere; on the walls there were paintings, her floor covered by a hand-designed and hand-hooked giant shag rug, in the corners there were sculptures. I was fascinated by the variety of art, all the little details, and how they were all different, but they all felt like her.

Everyone loved Aunt Bobbie. However, they were not supportive of her work as an artist. Others in the family did not see her art as a vocation, and she was a self-taught amateur. The family was full of scientists and business people, and the world Aunt Bobbie lived in was not their milieu.

Conversations regarding Aunt Bobbie filled me with ideas that creativity and art were silly hobbies with little meaning in the real world.

Many years later, when Aunt Bobbie rounded her 100th birthday, we looked through her art in the basement. We discussed why it was so important to her. She said art felt like an important force, and she always tried new things, which kept her curious and engaged throughout her entire life. She thought she would be making art until she died, which was the case.

Sitting in my office, I have a painting Aunt Bobbie made in the 1930s on my wall. I wish I had spent more time making art with her. Now, the more creative activity I engage in, whether painting, knitting, playing music, dancing, writing, or rug tufting, the better my work product becomes. She would be pleasantly surprised to see how much she inspires me and what creativity brings to my professional career.

Without creativity in the workplace, we find ourselves stuck. Stuck going down the same path over and over again. Stuck trying to get out of difficult situations with no resolution. Stuck doing what others do, losing differentiation. Stuck without understanding true needs.

As the winter of 2020 started, I decided to revisit creative activities, and my work improved. It turns out I was not the only one.

A few years before my pandemic languishing, I made a major career shift and took a national position as a C-suite clinical leader for a national healthcare organization known for innovation. Being C-suite meant I had a chief title, and I would work directly with the organization's senior leaders. I had a big seat at an important table, and I knew I would need help to transition into this role successfully. I was fortunate my boss at the time agreed. I connected with a talented young executive coach, Randi Braun. One of the most surprising parts of my work with her was a discovery concerning creativity. When I felt stuck, Randi challenged me to reengage with my own creativity. As a coach, Randi advises many clients who have struggled with feeling stuck in their careers.

"I think it's very ironic that companies are always asking employees to innovate, disrupt, or create. Because teams are never as big as they could be, because deadlines are always shorter than they have to be, we become packed at work with obligations that completely obstruct our ability to innovate, disrupt, and create. It's so obvious to me people need time for creativity," she said.

I was curious as to why Randi thought creativity was obvious. I have noticed with many friends and work colleagues as we age, we are more set in our ways. We are supposed to be *experts* in a few topics and stick to these topics. Companies hire us for jobs where we have already demonstrated the skillset for the position. We are supposed to *stay in our lane* at work.

Randi made a career transition a few years ago and is now the CEO of a rapidly growing coaching business called Something Major. As part of her transition, she reengaged with her creative side by combining her childhood passion for music and nature.

"For me, creativity tends to be the first thing that hits the chopping block when my day, month, or quarter gets busy. To drive new ideas, I need a creative brief every day. One can only describe this as a musical urban hike. I live near Rock Creek Park in Washington, DC, and you walk down a big hill from my house past iconic DC row houses.

"From the moment my feet hit the path, it is like a moving meditation. I put on a playlist and do some combination of singing, dancing, walking, and thinking. I perceive my brain is off. I am thinking about the woods. My feet and body know the way, and I'm kind of bopping along. At some point, something hits me. It is like a pot of water you have put on to boil, you step away, and I don't feel the bubble coming up. Then suddenly, it feels like a rolling boil, and I say, 'Oh my god, that's an idea!' or 'Oh my god, of course that's the answer!'

"And every big idea which has driven my business forward has come from this hike. When I get home, I sit in the crook of the stoop vestibule outside my door and stay there as long as I physically can before I go inside. I think and process and jot down my thoughts before I go inside.

"I am the CEO of a business that has grown hand over fist. I'm the mom of two young kids. I'm married to someone who is in a senior leadership role at a tech start-up. There is not a minute of unused time in my day. And for me, this carve out is truly one of the most important things of my life," she said.

Randi walked in nature to escape languishing and find flow. I shared with Randi how I hid my *play* activities from others, feeling silly or judged for things I enjoyed. Randi was not surprised. She sees this play out frequently with her clients, where the workplace frowns on creativity. She said:

"We live in this performative culture, where we do not celebrate creativity until you're like a famous artist like Yo-Yo Ma or JK Rowling. It's sad, right? Because we know from childhood education how important play is, and then at some point, the switch is flipped. We get the message—being creative or playful outside work is bad for our professional reputation. I think one of the biggest structural issues we have at work is that creativity is simply frowned upon. And what is celebrated? You have three extra things on your resume, or you were part of the business trip to go to Seattle. What is frowned upon? You went running in the middle of the day, or you took the time to play piano."

After talking with Randi, I was curious to learn more about creativity and its impact on problem-solving.

CHAPTER 2

Creativity and Flow

———

One of the unfortunate consequences of researching this book is—I don't eat octopus.

I have a newfound respect and sense of kinship for this mysterious creature. Like most people, I tend to think humans have all the answers. I learned the octopus could teach humans a great deal about creativity.

LEARNING FROM THE OCTOPUS

I read a few books on the octopus: *Metazoa* (Godfrey-Smith 2021), *The Soul of An Octopus* (Montgomery 2016), watched videos (Octolab TV 2022), and watched the documentary *My Octopus Teacher* (Erlich and Reed 2020). It fascinated me how the octopus loves to solve puzzles and will attempt to solve puzzles even when there is no clear incentive like food involved. Even though their neural system is different and much of their cognitive processes delegate to neural nets in their tentacles, they are puzzle-solvers by nature.

Similarly, humans have active minds and are always looking for ways to solve problems. Books like *When Brains Dream* (Zadra 2022) suggest the main reason we sleep is to help access more information within our brains to solve problems. *Human suffering can look like a mind which can't stop trying to solve problems.* Mindfulness and meditation are attempts to give us a break from endless problem-solving.

The octopus doesn't need to meditate. Since the octopus possesses neural nets in its tentacles, one arm can be off solving problems while another arm rests or minds the environment. Wouldn't it be great if we could do the same thing and delegate part of our brain to endless problem-solving while the other part of our brain rests? When I meditate, I feel a sensation of switching back and forth, like my brain briefly stops problem-solving, then it quickly flips back. Or the strange sensation: as soon as you are fully mindful, you see yourself being mindful, and you flip out of the mindful state.

Humans can reduce suffering by reframing constant problem-solving as a type of creative play. Like in the octopus videos, we can curiously test things and enjoy the process. If we creatively problem-solved at work, exploring, then wouldn't work feel more like play?

When work was more manual, did the repetitive movements allow the mind to shift gears into a more meditative space? Or was the mind still suffering and trying to solve problems related to money or other things? When I read books written hundreds or even thousands of years ago (like Marcus Aurelius' *Meditations*)—it appears the mind was constantly problem-solving, even though the nature of work was different from today.

Many science and art historians have found connections between creativity, play, science, and art. For example, Arthur Miller writes about the connections between the creative process, problem-solving, art, and science for Pablo Picasso and Albert Einstein in the early twentieth century (Miller 2002). Both Picasso and Einstein engaged in periods of individual deep work and stimulating intellectual social activities, finding inspiration in unexpected places.

The idea of *Deep Work* is the topic of the 2016 book of the same title by Cal Newport (Newport 2016). Deep work involves activities performed in a distraction-free state of concentration which pushes your cognitive capabilities to their limit. Deep work creates new value in our lives and the lives of others, improves skills, and specifically tackles difficult activities.

Having dedicated time for deep work was a key component of finding flow states for Picasso, but you don't need to be Picasso to benefit from flow. The idea of flow was elegantly described by the philosopher Mihaly Csikszentmihalyi in his 1990 book *Flow: The Psychology of Optimal Experience* (Csikszentmihalyi 2009). In his TEDx Talk, he proposes the key to happiness is increasing our flow states, whether through play, creative work, sports, music, reading, socializing, or even washing the dishes (TED 2008). The key is to give ourselves the time and space needed to get into flow—and it takes practice.

TIME CONFETTI IS KILLING YOUR CREATIVITY

When I decided to get creative in the winter of 2020, I had to find time for creative activities. I reached out again to Randi, who turned me on to the concept of **time confetti**. Brigid Schulte coined this term in her prepandemic book *Overwhelmed* (Schulte 2015). It explains why today's workers, especially women with families, feel constantly overwhelmed.

Time confetti is all the tiny bits of time sucked away by constant interruptions, often by our smart watches, phones, tablets, and laptops. She proposes that time confetti destroys our leisure time because we don't enjoy prolonged stretches of leisure, leading to a profound sense of overwhelm.

I looked at my days and found many examples of time confetti. Much of it was related to my devices and endless notifications and pings, but much of it was not related to screens. It was the tiny household tasks requiring five to fifteen minutes. It was scheduling kid events on a calendar. It was getting ready in the morning. It was eating lunch on the fly. When I reflected, I could see many examples of time confetti throughout my life. I realized I developed strategies that worked through careful time management, chunking tasks, and routines.

In college, I had zero internet and zero smartphones, and I still felt the pressure of time confetti. Typically overloaded with classes, homework, labs, and music practice, my freshman year was a muddle. Classes happened at different times on different days in different locations, and I found myself running all over campus with unused short breaks of time.

Over the next few years, I learned to cluster my classes during the same days and same locations. I learned where the libraries were, and if I had forty-five minutes free, I had a book to read with me. I learned how to schedule my labs in the afternoon so I could go directly from a long lab to music practice. I found ways to combine similar tasks and remove time confetti. My efficiency improved, and so did my grades.

Later, as parents of two small kids, my husband and I eliminated time confetti through routines. We had a tightly choreographed morning and evening routine. One parent got themselves ready for work while the other did wake up and breakfast. Then, the roles reversed. One parent got ready for work while the other got everyone out the door. In the evening, the routine was a tiring exercise in efficiency. Between 5–7 p.m., we drove home, ate dinner, cleaned up, bathed the children, prepared clothes for the next day, brushed teeth, combed hair, put on PJs, read multiple stories, and secured each child in their bed. I am tired just remembering this routine, but it worked. If we successfully pulled off the evening routine, we had two to three hours of me-time and spouse-time before bed.

Fast forward to winter 2020—I had forgotten all these skills from the past. I had to relearn chunking and routines (more to follow in chapter 3). When I got rid of the time confetti, I had time to start getting creative and start solving my problem of languishing.

CREATIVITY AT WORK

When researching ways to merge creativity and work, I thought of Dave Joseph. Dave worked in various settings in his career; before he started official *work* he was a drummer. Dave has found a way to combine his love of music and work. He is the owner and manager of a School of Rock franchise—teaching kids and their parents to love and understand rock music through lessons, bands, and performances.

Dave and his team had to draw upon their creative minds during the pandemic to solve new problems. Dave said:

"We were 100 percent online for three months. There was a lot of trial and error during that time. I think that's part of the creative process. You try something out to see if it works. You fine-tune it, modify it, and adjust it.

"Specifically, as it related to having kids' music lessons and band practices in a virtual setting, we had to figure out what sounded good on both ends of the connection. Everybody had different internet speeds and connection capabilities in their homes. For the drum instructors and drum students, we found an extra challenge because Zoom has a feature where if things get too loud, it clips the audio altogether.

"So, our drum lessons were a nightmare because everyone had their devices too close to the drum sets, and the audio cut out. Since the whole franchise School of Rock system was virtual at this time, somebody realized for drum lessons, it's better to have two devices, one close to the drum set to catch the video and the other one on the other side of the room to capture the audio. This was a great example of the creative process to solve a problem."

This statement really resonated with me because I see *creativity as a process to solve problems.* Creativity often takes someone else's ideas and tweaks them to solve a problem in a new way.

Dave shared with me a funny story about how this has played out in his own life. Like me, Dave finds it fun to solve problems in creative ways. Dave said:

"Throughout my career, I found great satisfaction and joy and pleasure in taking on newly created roles. Maybe it was a new division, a new department, or taking on roles in spots where things had gone completely sideways, and they needed somebody to come in with a fresh set of eyes. I would come in and look at it differently and ask, 'If you were building it from scratch and throwing out everything done in the past, how would you approach it?'"

I asked Dave for an example. He said:

"One of the first times I took someone else's idea and modified it slightly to make it better was in 1987. I was president of my fraternity in college and trying to figure out how to get all the guys to attend the weekly meeting. I talked to someone who led a different fraternity, and he said, 'I have a deck of cards, and every time you come to a meeting, we hand out a card as we take attendance. Over the course of five meetings, you have a poker hand, and the guy with the best poker hand wins a case of beer.' I thought: that's genius—a great solution doesn't cost a lot.

"At that time, I went to Las Vegas, and at one of the little gift shops at a casino, I bought a deck of *Playboy* playing cards. I took these cards back to the fraternity and handed them out for attendance. We played poker with the cards. More importantly, all the fellows got a kick out of seeing which card they would get at a particular meeting. The images on the cards amped it up a bit."

Dave smiled, and his face lit up. Chuckling, he said:

"The best part of this story was that in the fall, I used this story in an interview for a real job going into the retail industry. When the HR person asked me, 'Have you ever taken somebody else's idea and improved upon it?' I told her the story about these playing cards. It was a risk to talk about that in a formal interview. You're not sure how people will react. I went for it, and I saw the smile on this person's face as I was telling the story. I struck a chord, and I was being my genuine self. You can be creative if you allow yourself the latitude to try not to necessarily conform all the time."

What I love most about this story is how the creative mindset was applied to the initial problem—getting the fraternity guys to come to meetings—and took it up a notch with the naughty playing cards. Then Dave showed another layer of creativity by applying this story to a job interview.

I can imagine so clearly the smile on the HR interviewer's face when a young Dave shared the story. He used emotional impact—the humor of the naughty cards—to show his ability to connect with customers in a tangible way. I am not surprised Dave got the job.

In the future of work, this type of creativity is key. When the pace of work is fast and the tools of work are rapidly changing, the ability to take a good idea and tweak it is a great skill. Seeing a situation with fresh eyes can often lead to radical simplification. Connecting it all back to emotional impact, particularly humor, really motivates humans to get the job done.

BURN THE TIME CONFETTI AND REDISCOVER PLAY

Most people experienced languishing during the pandemic, a strange sense of disconnected time with little play and little meaning. If you are still stuck languishing, it is not too late to escape.

Identifying and reducing time confetti permits longer uninterrupted periods of time. During this time, we can use play and creativity to enter flow states. Flow helps us feel reconnected with our lives and the people surrounding us. Long stretches of uninterrupted work are called deep work and will allow us to focus on the big problems at work rather than get caught up in time confetti.

Decreasing languishing, increasing play, increasing flow, and increasing creativity all help our brains function better and generate a much more pleasurable state of being. This type of brain state is linked to creative problem-solving and helps us spend less time working, generating more efficient and effective work. Time for creative problem-solving doesn't happen automatically.

CHAPTER 3

Saying No and Boundaries

The fear of missing out—FOMO—is our new enemy.

Virtual work led to a breakdown of boundaries between home and work. People felt distressed, exhausted, and confused. To create time for deep work, creativity, and flow, we must set new boundaries and learn how to say no.

THE DEATH OF FOMO

On a chilly pandemic Saturday in December 2020, I curled up on the couch with nothing to do. I turned on Netflix and started a mindless scroll through recommended shows. I was languishing, and even though it was the weekend, I didn't have much to look forward to.

As I thought about what my family and friends were doing, I had a sudden realization—everyone was probably doing the same thing. They were probably sitting on their couch, mindlessly scrolling.

Prepandemic, December was an extraordinarily busy time of year. A normal December overwhelmed me between holiday parties, getting ready for Christmas, multiple family birthday parties, New Year's Eve, and wrapping up business fiscal year activities. Often, we would find multiple events on the same day and have to turn down invitations. I normally had a sense I forgot something or I didn't get to do all the things I wanted to.

I remember feeling a sense of extreme **FOMO—fear of missing out** during the holiday season. The pandemic effectively killed FOMO because there were no more birthday parties to attend and no more social events. We all sat at home binge-watching *Tiger King*. This got me thinking—did I really miss those holiday parties? I realized I mindlessly said yes to all the holiday events due to FOMO rather than because I actually enjoyed the events themselves.

One of the best things to come out of the pandemic is a questioning of our assumptions around busyness. We have a better sense of what is important to us and what is not important. We are in a unique position to hold our boundaries. We can say no to things that are not important to us, set boundaries, and keep FOMO at bay. In my holiday party example, I realized for the future holiday seasons 2021, 2022, 2023, etc., I could intentionally say yes to the holiday events which were meaningful or enjoyable and say no to the rest. I could set better boundaries and keep my FOMO under control.

Perhaps it will not surprise you to learn that psychologists have been studying FOMO for years (Hobson 2018). Behavioral scientists have a technical term for FOMO—**regret aversion**. Regret aversion means fearing regret from either a) doing or b) not doing an action (The Decision Lab 2022). Richard Mathera is a managing director at Irrational Labs, a company specializing in behavioral science (Irrational Labs 2022). When I asked to explain the relationship between FOMO and regret aversion, he said:

"I think it's reasonable to consider FOMO as a specific case of regret aversion in which you fear regret from not taking an action. Most often, an action you perceive others are taking or would have taken."

It turns out—regret aversion powerfully motivates human behavior. We are more motivated to do something because we have regret aversion than if we actually receive a reward for the behavior. In my example above, I attended holiday parties because I had regret aversion of *not* going to the party. FOMO overpowered my actual enjoyment of the party. Often, I attended parties I did not enjoy.

Researchers have studied regret aversion in a variety of settings, including health behaviors and real estate (Brewer 2016; Seiler 2008). They all find the same thing. Humans can be highly irrational, saying yes to things that are not logically in their best interests due to regret aversion/FOMO. This psychology is used for good—and for bad. You have probably purchased something as a *limited edition* because of the regret aversion, worrying you would miss out on buying it in the future.

Even prepandemic, many people were taking a closer look at FOMO and how it led to a decrease in happiness. During the pandemic, I listened to the audiobook *The Subtle Art of Not Giving a F*ck: A Counterintuitive Approach to Living a Good Life* by Mark Manson (Manson 2016). I have a confession. I randomly selected this audiobook based solely on the provocative title with f*ck in it, as well as the high reader ratings (currently 4.5/5 stars with 123,576 ratings). What was all the fuss about?

I expected to listen to a rant against hard work, achievement, and drive: a recommendation to sit back, take it easy, and smell the roses. I got something entirely different. Mark's premise: to really and truly care about something and make a difference, you have to stop caring about other things, stop being distracted by things that don't really matter and stop being blocked by your own fears of failure. Mark said:

"The key to a good life is not giving a f*ck about more; it's giving a f*ck about less, giving a f*ck about only what is true and immediate and important."

The book also made a powerful argument—if you can stop giving a f*ck about things that don't matter, it will help you get rid of FOMO and focus on the things which really do matter. Killing FOMO is not a new concept. It is common sense. However, in the age of smart sales engines and artificial intelligence in apps like Instagram, the world creates a state of FOMO all around you.

The psychology of regret aversion plays a powerful role in why traditional work sucks, and researchers are interested in how FOMO plays out in the workplace. A 2019 study showed FOMO in the workplace is real and it has a distinct impact on employee well-being (Budnick 2020). At work, the researchers found two kinds of FOMO: 1) social comparisons with other employees and 2) valuable workplace opportunities. They said:

"[Workplace FOMO] is the pervasive apprehension that, relative to other employees, one might miss valuable career opportunities when away or disconnected from work. FOMO at work should manifest as the fear of missing opportunities for rewarding experiences like building professional relationships, gaining valuable information, and contributing to key organizational decisions and projects."

Not surprisingly, they found workplace FOMO correlated with increased message-checking behaviors, increased burnout, and decreased employee psychological well-being. Of note, workplace FOMO increased message-checking but did not increase engagement with work. In other words, when you are at work, if you have FOMO, you will frequently check your emails, DMs, texts, and Slack more and more. However, you will experience less and less positive engagement with your work. Does this sound familiar?

Researchers are also starting to explore the way our brains process regret aversion. In one study, they scanned people's brains while they were playing a gambling game (Coricelli 2005). In this game, the researchers inserted regret aversion to motivate people to make more irrational gambling choices. They found as the experiment progressed, the individuals became increasingly regret-aversive, experiencing more and more FOMO. This FOMO reflects in enhanced brain activity within two areas of the brain: the medial orbitofrontal cortex and amygdala. This FOMO pattern of activity reoccurred *before* making a choice, suggesting the same brain pathways are responsible for both the direct experience of regret *and* its anticipation.

I am interested in this tight connection between an older part of the human brain related to emotions (amygdala) and a newer part of the brain (the medial orbitofrontal cortex), which uses a higher brain *thinking* process to determine the value of a potential outcome (Gorley 2016). In other words, when you are trying to decide whether to say yes or no to something, the emotional part of your brain syncs up with the thinking part of your brain to decide—do I want to make that choice?

To simplify, FOMO turns up the emotional component of the choice (amygdala). When a strong feeling of FOMO occurs, the emotional brain overrides the more logical thinking component of the choice (medial orbitofrontal cortex). We make irrational decisions, we say yes to things even when we know we should say no.

BOUNDARIES ARE THE NEW "NO"

In 2010, I opened my own private psychiatry practice, and I made all the rules. I wanted my patients to have full access to me. Sometimes I responded back to an email instantly. Sometimes I took a phone call at 9 p.m. Sometimes, I sent in a prescription when a patient asked for it rather than when I thought they needed it.

At first, this worked great. My patients loved my instant responses, and I gave them what they were asking for. After six months, things weren't so great. I had poor boundaries around my time, and as the number of patients in my practice grew, it became intrusive. I found myself frantically checking email between appointments and dashing off responses without pausing to gather my thoughts. I found myself taking phone calls at all hours of the night and on the weekends. I found that sometimes I prescribed a desired medication which was not really the best choice for the patient.

As I continued to add patients in 2011, I knew something had to change. My boundaries sucked, and as a result, my work sucked too. I saw something interesting—my patients were not doing great either. Because we hadn't agreed upon any boundaries for our work together, they felt distressed. They didn't know what to expect from me. If I responded to an email after three hours instead of three minutes, they worried something was wrong and got anxious. If I didn't respond to an after-hours phone call because I was doing something at home, they got worried, then anxious, then upset, and their mood escalated into a bad state.

I realized the process of setting boundaries was an important part of the patient-doctor relationship. With consistent and thoughtful boundaries, I conveyed empathy, professionalism, and competency. I talked to other psychiatrists and learned how boundary setting was a collaborative expectation-setting exercise that built trust between the patient and the doctor. I revamped my practice boundaries. I practiced doing the boundary-setting exercise collaboratively with patients.

Over the years, this strategy succeeded. After growing my private practice to include other psychiatrists and administrative staff, it became even more important to clarify and maintain boundaries across a population of 800 plus active patients. I codified the boundaries in our operations manual, and we trained on the boundary-setting process collaboratively with patients.

In all the different places I worked, with all the different leaders I coached, and the clients I consulted with, *I have rarely seen this type of collaborative boundary setting in the workplace.* Typically, I have seen either 1) silent, assumed, and social norms, 2) highly structured employee manuals which are on paper but not followed in reality, or 3) explicit team-based norms that are variable across the organization.

Without explicit **collaborative boundary setting** in the workplace, employees feel like my patients. They are worried they are doing something wrong, anxious when they don't hear back immediately, moody and depressed because they feel they do not have the ability to say no. Humans feel a general lack of control when the boundaries are vague.

Another popular phrase for me growing up in the 1980s came from Nancy Reagan, who famously said: Just say no. **Just say no** became the slogan for public service announcements encouraging kids to say away from drugs. In the same way that saying no is difficult for kids faced with drugs, it is difficult to say no to distractions at work.

Peer pressure at work can be powerful. Observing other people or your boss working on things that don't matter, being distracted by never-ending emails, or spending long hours on perfecting PowerPoint presentations—we surrender to the social pressure of the status quo. As humans, the behavior of our social circle strongly influences us. Psychologists have researched this phenomenon of social norms for many years (Mcleod 1970).

Social norms are collective beliefs regarding what kind of behavior is appropriate in a given situation. They are unwritten and provide us with an expectation of how we should behave. American culture values the idea of the individual, so Americans are in a tricky situation. We undervalue the power of social norms, and therefore, social pressures are invisible and we internalize them. This plays out in a variety of ways in the workplace.

Prepandemic, what were common American social norms at work? We commuted, sometimes for hours a day. We sat in a physical office from at least 9 a.m.–5 p.m. We worked in offices, cubicles, or sometimes in open floor plans. We indicated status by office location, office size, and furniture. We used email and expected a response quickly. Face time with the boss or leadership was a closely guarded commodity, with boundaries of assistants, office walls, and difficult-to-reach locations. Most boundaries were physical, and we typically made friends with the people physically located close to us. This phenomenon is known as the **law of propinquity** (Sugihto 2016).

During the pandemic, physical boundaries at work disappeared. Kids and pets started appearing on video meetings. Emails stretched to twenty-four seven. On the

Hollywood-Squares-Zoom calls, the boss looked the same size and location as everyone else on the call. This blurring of boundaries created an opportunity for new social norms at work to emerge. Unfortunately, in many cases, the social norms drifted into a twenty-four seven work cycle where people were neither 100 percent at work nor 100 percent at home, causing confusion, and distress. One study found that first-time remote workers had high rates of depression (17.9 percent), anxiety (19.6 percent), and stress (19.6 percent). Rates were highest among women and people who were having difficulty sleeping (Şentürk 2012). Another study of young people during COVID-19 found over 70 percent of the respondents had greater than moderate levels of stress, with 59 percent meeting the criteria for clinically significant anxiety and 39 percent reporting moderate depressive symptoms (Varma 2021).

At the time of this writing, the pandemic is in an endemic stage. Companies are trying to figure out the new normal, and we have an opportunity to create healthier social norms at work. Start-ups have the luxury of creating a new culture with new boundaries from scratch. Most companies need to find ways to make small steps toward a more positive workplace. What small steps make it easier to minimize distractions, focus on what is important, set boundaries, and just say no?

1. Say no to working vacations and during days off
Say yes to taking all your vacation.
Say yes to preparing your team for your vacation.
Say yes to planning backup for when you are on vacation and help others as a backup for their vacation.

Set *unplugged* status during vacation, no email, no DM, no meetings, nothing.

If necessary to work on a day off or while on vacation, delay schedule all communication to go out to other people when back in the office, not on unplugged time.

Put an out-of-office message on all communication channels (email, phone, DM) and indicate who the backup is and how they can reach that person.

2. Say no to meetings which can be emails or other asynchronous work
Say yes to asking, "Why do we need this meeting?"
Say yes to asking, "Who needs to attend this meeting?"
Set boundaries and norms around communication during meetings (see the communication section of this book).
Say yes to investing in asynchronous work tools.

3. Say no to instant email culture
Say yes to *batching* emails and sending them out once in the morning and once in the afternoon.
Turn off email notifications.
Close email when not batching responses.
Let people know when to expect email checks and offer urgent contact options like text messages or phone calls.

4. Say no to staring at a box from 9 a.m.–5 p.m.
Say yes to taking breaks.
Say yes to standing up and moving around.
Find ways to work flexibly during times of optimal cognitive performance.

As a leader or manager of other people, it is much easier to create new social norms. Leaders can plan for it, discuss it, execute it, and monitor it.

If you are a leader or manager, *one of your biggest challenges will be to follow the rules yourself* and model the behavior you want to see in your team. You will probably feel the temptation to *cheat* and respond back to emails immediately or to check in with a team member during your day off. There are plenty of hacks you can use to hold yourself accountable.

One of my favorites is to schedule emails. If I am tempted or, by necessity, have to check email outside of my weekday routine, I do not send a response back, no matter what. I schedule the email to go out when I would normally be on my weekday routine, so I preserve the social norm of checking email during the routine.

CHUNKING AND CHECKING

When I think of the article on workplace FOMO and the constant message-checking behaviors, it reminds me of a young man I worked with in my psychiatry practice. Tim (not his real name) was in his early thirties and grew up with a variety of challenges, including learning disorders and severe obsessive-compulsive disorder (OCD).

OCD is an extreme manifestation of 1) an internal anxiety state with distressing obsessive thought loops, and 2) repetitive external behaviors that help reduce the internal sense of anxiety.

As an adult, Tim lived alone in an apartment next to his mother's home, and he had persistent internal thoughts and anxiety something was wrong at his apartment. To alleviate this anxiety, he performed a variety of checking behaviors like turning the stove on and off twenty times, opening and closing a door twenty times, or touching a window twenty times.

With psychotherapy treatment, Tim learned to recognize and understand his OCD, but he could not turn it off. With medication, his anxiety decreased enough for him to create short chunks of time for him to complete his checking routines. He spent ten minutes on a checking routine in the morning before he left for work and another ten minutes in the evening before he went to bed. We measured success by the number of anxious phone calls to his mother.

Without medication, Tim would engage in checking activities for up to an hour in the morning, making him late for work. He would have been checking things at night and unable to fall asleep for hours. In other words, untreated OCD and checking behaviors would have made him nonfunctional and unable to support himself.

The idea behind **chunking** is simple—you chunk together similar tasks in a set amount of time *to minimize task shifting*. This helps your brain focus on the task at hand and not jump around to other tasks (see multitasking in chapter 1). You then create **routines** where these chunks are lined up in a predictable, repetitive fashion so your brain knows what to expect and can start to go on autopilot.

By having routines, you decrease the number of cognitive decisions you must make throughout the day—should I do A or B next? Chunking and routines are powerful tools to improve your day-to-day experience at work.

Michael Hyatt is a guru of time management and efficiency at work, and his system Free To Focus (Free To Focus 2022), is a great tool for understanding chunking and routine. I love how Michael framed time management. He said:

"Making appointments with yourself and scheduling other things around them is key to proactive self-management."

After completing his book, I realized I needed to set a big boundary: no meetings after 3 p.m.

FIND THE WHY

Setting boundaries is hard. We can use tools to help navigate difficult conversations, and we can use tech tools to put boundaries around our time. *For most people, the hardest part of setting boundaries is identifying what your boundaries are and the why behind the boundary.* Without the why, we are not firm in our own minds about what is important to us and what we are not giving a f*ck about.

I learned over time that my brain function hits a natural lull in my circadian rhythm at this time, and I feel slowed, irritable, and not in the mood to talk with other people. I have found this boundary difficult to maintain because, naturally, other people's brains work just great at 3 p.m., and they want to meet during this time.

For me to keep this boundary, I have to constantly connect back to *why* the boundary exists in the first place. The obvious *why*: I don't function well at 3 p.m. The deeper *why*—what will happen when I take a meeting at 3 p.m.? I will show up to the meeting in a bad frame of mind, and my energy will affect the other person in the meeting. They will get a worse version of me. My negative energy will follow them through their day. I 100 percent cannot actively listen if I am irritable and in a bad frame of mind, so I talk over people, zone out, or interrupt and give unsolicited advice.

By connecting to the superficial why and the deeper why of not meeting past 3 p.m., I can say no to these meetings. Please understand saying no remains a daily challenge for me. Many times, I slip or have to make an exception. To keep myself accountable, I have a weekly check where I go through my calendar for the upcoming week and look for any meetings after 3 p.m. If a meeting has slipped onto my schedule, I consider it carefully. If not needed, I reach out to the meeting organizer and let them know I cannot attend and suggest an alternative approach.

I see chicken-and-egg phenomena here with myself and my coaching clients. When we have no time to ourselves to sit and think, it is difficult to know what is truly important to us and what boundaries are meaningful.

So, to find my why, I take a few steps. I first carve out a little time once a week for an hour to go to a quiet place, turn off notifications, tell others not to disturb me, take a piece of paper, and think. I think about what matters to me and what doesn't matter. I write it down.

Once solid in what is important to you, write it down. Say it aloud with confidence. Then, and only then, plan those boundaries and difficult conversations. You may need to put it in writing everyday or practice saying it aloud. Maybe you'll even be tempted to say, "Well, this isn't important."

Returning to my example—the boundary of not scheduling meetings past 3 p.m.—I am continually tempted to break this boundary, especially when my colleagues live in a different time zone. If they are on the West Coast, it means no meetings past noon their time. This temptation also occurs when the meeting is with a large group of people, and I know they all have tricky schedules. Here are things I do to avoid temptation:

1. Use an automatic calendar to schedule meetings. I program different types of meetings with automatic boundaries attached for time, day, and length. This keeps me in control of what I am saying yes to and no to automatically, avoiding many conversations where there would be a temptation for me to say yes.
2. Not responding to email or calendar invites right away. I chunk emails and respond once in the morning and once in the evening. This gives me time between looking at the invite and making a decision, often making it easier to say no.
3. Asking for more information. Often, meetings appear without context or an agenda. If I don't know the details, I ask for the goal of the meeting. Often, I don't really need a meeting. A quick chat or asynchronous communication will achieve the same goal. Or I only need fifteen minutes

instead of sixty minutes. Or I find someone else better suited to attend the meeting.

4. Finally, on a weekly basis, I review the meetings for the upcoming week. If I have said yes to something I should have said no to, I reach out and ask the person to reschedule. If not, I look for ways to shorten the meeting or do the prep work asynchronously so we can make it quick.

Despite all these tips and tricks, I still fall prey to temptation—I am human too. However, I am better at holding important boundaries, and I continue to improve.

When I thought about setting boundaries in the virtual world, I immediately thought of Mike. I first met Mike at a particularly low point in his life when he needed a psychiatrist to help him manage his medications and make sense of his situation. When I caught up with Mike recently, he was thriving.

Mike explained to me the system he created to minimize FOMO and say yes to the things which matter most. He said:

"I have a few rules that I follow, and I keep it simple. I don't engage in any forums where there are groups of people all talking to one another. I only have one-on-one conversations with people, and I only use the phone if I want to talk to someone.

"I used to read many programming newsletters online, and I saw they were negatively impacting me—sending me constant messages of 'you're failing' over and over. In a way, they act like they're gonna teach you something, but this implies you're not doing enough, you haven't learned enough, you are failing, or you need to read this article. Once I shut off all these other sites, then my confidence went through the roof.

"Another thing my mentor taught me was the importance of positive messages. Now my house is covered in written positive messages. I sometimes will still go on Reddit, where people will ask me questions about my work. When I go there, I ignore all the ugly stuff. If somebody's got something nice to say, I'll answer their question, and I will only say good stuff. What I see now is that when I send out only good stuff, now all I get back is good stuff."

Despite living alone and rarely leaving his house, Mike feels more connected than ever. He feels he has greater meaning in his life through his connections, and his work has a greater impact because he only focuses on two things: having fun and to make his users successful.

Mike crushed FOMO because he said yes to what mattered and no to what didn't matter.

SUMMARY
One of the most positive outcomes of the pandemic was the death of FOMO. We no longer assume we have to say yes to everything. We have the opportunity to get out of the bad habits of the past, where the psychological trap of regret aversion drove us to overcommit to things that lacked value and meaning.

One of the hardest parts about avoiding FOMO and regret aversion in the workplace is setting boundaries. Most workplace cultures have operated on norms and assumptions without collaborative boundary setting as a team. There is no right or wrong answer when it comes to boundary setting. However, people need time to unplug, rest, recharge, play, and be creative.

In this chapter, I shared a personal example of boundary setting in the workplace and tips and strategies for chunking and routines which help with setting boundaries. Up next, I will take a closer look at our cult of busyness and time management strategies to improve the workplace.

CHAPTER 4

Time Management Strategies and Technology

———

Most of us are cult members and we don't even know it. The *cult of busyness* has become entrenched in American culture. Many people find joy in checking off to-do lists, and the way we spend our leisure time makes us less happy. We feel a sense of something being wrong. We don't know how to fix it, and our brains are not getting enough time to play and rest.

Luckily, there are many tools to improve our time management. Many of the same tools that caused a breakdown of boundaries can create new and healthier boundaries and habits. The key is aggressively and intentionally building these new habits using technology designed for real humans.

MY CHECKBOX ADDICTION

My addiction to busyness started when I was a junior in high school. Eager to travel outside my small town in Pennsylvania and see the world, my parents told me I should start saving money to fund my travel overseas.

I took on any work I could find. During the school year, I worked a newspaper delivery route, the layaway/gift wrap counter at a department store, waitressed at Howard Johnson's restaurant, and babysat. During the summers, I lived at a family beach house and worked 7 a.m.–12 p.m. at a children's clothing store, went to the beach from 12–5 p.m., showered, ate dinner, then went back to work from 7–10 p.m.

Every day I had a long list of checkboxes of things to do, and I got really good at managing my time and checking off the boxes. The rewards were clear—after I saved enough money, I would spend it all on travel overseas. These time-management strategies and box-checking held me in good stead through college, working part-time jobs, studying like crazy, and still saving money for travel, while also banking good grades for the future. I got a thrill from this skill because I could see and feel the future benefits of getting through my to-do list.

The pinnacle of checking boxes came for me in 2004 during my intern year at Mount Sinai Hospital in New York City. As a newly minted MD, I woke up at 4 a.m. every morning, walked uphill to the hospital, and started an endless list of things to do at 5 a.m. I had hundreds of tasks to complete each day, and if I missed a task, it could be literally a life-or-death mistake for one of my patients. The stakes were high; every minute used, nothing wasted.

After mastering a sign-out system to keep track of to-dos and check off all my boxes during my shift, I gained a new sense of mastery and accomplishment. Checking off these boxes led to meaningful outcomes for my patients and my team. Failing to complete my to-do list meant something bad could happen to a patient or leaving a team member in the lurch.

A few years later, I married and had my first child in the middle of my psychiatry residency training. Quickly the joy of checking boxes on the to-do list at work expanded into the checkboxes for parenthood and taking care of a baby. A new job brought new checkboxes. A second child brought new checkboxes. I heard myself respond to the question "how are you?" with "things are crazy busy..." Everyone else around me was saying the same thing. Work was busy, kids were busy, taking care of a household was busy, and social events were busy. Without knowing it, I had become part of the cult of busyness.

THE CULT OF BUSYNESS

Researchers discussed busyness over a hundred years ago. In 1899, the Norwegian American economist and sociologist Thorstein Veblen wrote *The Theory of the Leisure Class* (Veblen 1961). This text described the importance of wasteful leisure time at the turn of the century. He proposed that status and reputation were signaled by a rise in conspicuous leisure time and wasteful activities, demonstrating that wealth no longer required work. This signaling helped wealthy people in the merchant class appear similar to old money, aristocrats who lived off their titles and family money.

From 1894 through 1915, the Progressive Movement led to better working conditions, and even factory workers had an increase in leisure time. Workers participated in activities like sports, outdoor activities, and urban entertainment (The Library of Congress 2022). Wealthy Americans paid no income tax until 1913. The tax system known to us today did not become fully developed until the 1930s, and the rich had plenty of money to spend (Fontinelle 2022). Prior to the Great Depression, leisure was a highly desirable activity among the *new rich,* and the malaise of conspicuous leisure and conspicuous consumption of luxury goods was visible in books like *The Great Gatsby,* written in 1925 by F. Scott Fitzgerald (Fitzgerald 1925).

After the Great Depression, taxation of the rich continued to rise, with a peak marginal income tax rate of 94 percent in 1944. Combined with less disposable income and a wartime economy, the mindset of Americans shifted. Leisure stopped being a desirable goal—industry, efficiency, outcomes—all became the social norm. Postwar America saw economic growth and taxes decreased. The culture of industry and efficiency continued to evolve and mature.

Fast forward fifty years. In American culture, leisure was out of style. "I am so busy" became the new American mantra.

The **cult of busyness** gained traction in news articles and blog posts in the late 2000s (Muti 2007; Berkun 2021). A *Wall*

Street Journal article described the acceleration of busyness in American culture. It said:

"Words and phrases that began surfacing in the 1970s and 1980s—'hectic,' 'whirlwind,' 'consumed,' 'crazy,' 'constantly on the run,' and 'way too fast'—now appear with astonishing frequency" (Schulte 2014).

The author of this article, Brigid Schulte, was intrigued by this phenomenon and how she saw it play out in her own life. She continued to research and write, eventually publishing her book on the topic of busyness in 2015—*Overwhelmed: Work, Love, And Play When No One Has the Time* (Schulte 2015). By then, the American cult of busyness hit full force. Brigid said:

"*Overwhelmed* is a book about time pressure and modern life. It is a deeply reported and researched, honest and often hilarious journey from feeling that, as one character in the book said, 'time is like a *rabid lunatic* running naked and screaming as your life flies past you' to understanding the historical and cultural roots of the overwhelm, how worrying about all there is to do and the pressure of feeling like we'll never have enough time to do it all, or do it well, is *contaminating* our experience of time, how time pressure and stress is resculpting our brains and shaping our workplaces, our relationships and squeezing the space that the Greeks said was the point of living a good life: that elusive moment of peace called leisure."

An investigative journalist, Brigid took a deep look at the research and did her own fieldwork, interviewing Americans and looking at other cultures for clues. She concluded that Americans are addicted to busyness which creates great unhappiness in our culture. She left journalism to focus on making work better, and prepandemic created a toolkit called The Better Work Toolkit (New America 2022). Later in this chapter, we will take a closer look at this toolkit and how we can use it today.

After several years of experimenting with working from home during the pandemic, Americans are still struggling with the cult of busyness and the idea of leisure. A 2021 *BBC* article describes how busyness has become a status symbol. In a complete reversal from the early 1900s (Imtiaz 2021). It said:

"Those who complain the most about not having enough free time are wealthy and educated" (Hamermesh 2007).

In the last chapter, we saw why the brain needs play to stay nimble and adaptive. Play is one type of positive activity one can do during leisure time. Importantly, our brains also need time to rest and recharge. Escaping the cult of busyness is hard work. However, there are signs that the pandemic may have finally shaken us out of busyness (Love 2021). Tools like meditation can help.

MEDITATION IS A BRAIN HACK

A 2013 article in *Scientific American* summarizes the science of why we need breaks—naps, meditation, nature walks, etc.— to enter into a restful brain state which activates our **default mode network** (DMN) (Jabr 2013). While somewhat mysterious, researchers first observed this whole-brain oscillatory electrical activity pattern in the mid-1990s. At this time, the researcher Marcus Raichle of Washington University in Saint Louis noticed a particular set of scattered brain regions (the DMN) that consistently became less active when someone concentrated on a mental challenge. These same brain regions began to fire in synchrony as a subject lay flat in an fMRI brain scanner, their thoughts wandering.

Since then, research on the DMN has increased. Researchers have been finding that activation of the DMN while resting, relaxing, and daydreaming may be critical to a variety of brain functions. The DMN may be responsible for processing information, focusing on personal identity, accessing creativity, and having those a-ha moments when we are showering or doing other restful activities.

Remember Randi's story from chapter 1? She takes long walks in nature to enter a flow state. As a result of the flow state, she experiences a-ha moments that are critical to her work. Randi activates her DMN and gets creative on her nature walks.

As a neuroscientist and a recent fan of meditation, I believe meditation lets us watch our own DMN in action. A fascinating study done at Yale in 2011 showed mindfulness and meditation decreases activity in our DMN and decreases the self-referential *monkey mind* activity of the DMN (Brewer 2011). Meditation has many positive effects like an increase in connection to others, decrease in anxiety, helping with addiction, and improving brain function with age.

Earlier, I described my experience with meditation. I struggle to meditate for long periods of time, but on a typical day, I use an app to meditate for five to ten minutes. During this time, I experience odd moments of watching my thoughts, followed by an awareness that I am watching my thoughts, followed by a flip back into my thoughts. When I meditate, I am watching my DMN. However, my DMN quickly reasserts control and pulls me back into *my* thoughts. Meditation is a brain hack that both calms and frustrates me.

What if our cult of busyness hacks our brains to escape DMN *me* activity by turning on an endless set of external tasks? We may have created a new problem by trying to solve the essential human monkey mind feeling. If we turn to meditation and mindfulness instead as a way to monitor and modulate the DMN, our brains have the best of both worlds. We can experience both the me-centered processing of the DMN and the other-centered connectedness of meditation/mindfulness. By combining these strategies, we could finally escape the psychological pull of the cult of busyness.

PSYCHOLOGICAL TRAPS AT WORK

I enjoyed working with adults with attention deficit hyperactivity disorder (ADHD) in my private practice. As adults, they were less impaired by the hyperactivity part of ADHD. However, they exhibited serious problems with impulsivity and distraction. One young man had to schedule his college classes to evenings because he couldn't get up on time and would run hours late, failing all his morning classes. One middle-aged man missed all his client appointments and lost business. One young woman almost failed to get her graduate degree because she could not forecast study and writing time.

As I worked with more adult ADHD patients and attended annual conferences of APSARD—The American Professional Society of ADHD and Related Disorders—I learned adults with ADHD struggled greatly with time management at work. They were impulsive and would feel tempted to do low-priority fun tasks. They would easily be distracted while trying to get important tasks done. Adults with ADHD experienced time fluidly and had great difficulty forecasting how long it would take to finish tasks. They would typically underestimate how long it took to finish a task and overestimate how long it took to finish unpleasant tasks.

I knew there must be a tech solution to this problem, so in 2011 I designed and built an early app called CP on Time. This simple app asked a few simple questions to gauge the severity of adult ADHD: the tasks to complete in the morning (like getting dressed, eating breakfast, etc.), the distance traveled, and the time of the first meeting or appointment of the day. Using a simple algorithm, the app would then generate the time the person needed to get up in the morning and set the alarm on their phone. Typically, it added 50 percent time needed to get ready in the morning for mild ADHD, 100 percent of the time for moderate ADHD, and 150 percent of the time for severe ADHD. So, if you were an adult with severe ADHD and you had to be at work at 9 a.m. and had a commute of fifteen minutes and you thought it took you forty-five minutes to get ready in the morning, the app would set your alarm for 6:30 a.m.

When I used this app with patients, they were shocked. They didn't understand why the app told them to add so much extra time to their morning routine. They could not accept they were so wildly off with their ability to forecast time. Ultimately, the app failed, and I turned it off in 2014 because I dumped the app on patients and consumers without actually teaching them *why* they needed to use it. I forgot an important piece of psychoeducation—I needed to teach patients the **planning fallacy**—a common human psychological trap.

As mentioned earlier in this chapter, Brigid Schulte researches human time management at work. As part of her The Better Work Toolkit, she identifies a few key psychological traps at work. She said:

"Are you finding in your virtual workplace that your workday has extended into the evening?

"If so, you may be falling prey to the planning fallacy. Humans are notoriously bad at predicting their own futures and often fail to anticipate how long tasks will take to complete. In planning their schedules, workers may overestimate how much they can actually do in a day, which, in a flexible environment, can extend the workday into the evening and consume mental bandwidth with worry about how to get it all done or guilt when the day ends and the task remains undone.

"Are you procrastinating tasks at work?

"If so, you might have difficulty with **affective forecasting.** Humans underestimate how much emotional and physical states will affect their future decisions. In procrastinating or putting off work in the moment, workers may assume they'll be fantastically productive in the future and not take into account that they may feel exhausted, distracted, or unmotivated when it comes time to actually do work in the future.

"Are you checking your email constantly throughout the day?

"If so, you might be experiencing **network effects.** Working flexibly forfeits the gains when workers work at the same time and in the same place and taxes individual attention. To coordinate, workers rely more on email at all hours. To compensate for knowledge gaps and because humans are neurologically attuned to novelty, workers feel driven to check email constantly, in part to signal their commitment to work."

I believe the planning fallacy causes the most problems in the virtual/hybrid workplace. Like my ADHD patients, we all have difficulty planning our schedules in a flexible environment, leading to a breakdown of boundaries. We feel overwhelmed as we try frantically to check all the boxes on an endless to-do list. Many people attribute this to virtual/hybrid work. However, we were struggling with this sense of overwhelm, barrier breakdown, and endless to-do list before the pandemic introduced the masses to virtual work.

The Better Work Toolkit describes this challenge in prepandemic terms:

"In many work environments, flexibility is still viewed as a privilege for a chosen few. So, workers with flexible schedules and remote work tend to put in longer hours, viewing the time as an accommodation or gift. Because work can spread across twenty-four hours, seven days a week, boundaries between work and home can dissolve. Work and emails spill over into time and space once reserved for being "off" to rest, recover, and live the rest of life. Now, Americans work more odd hours, nights, and weekends than workers in other countries. The mere anticipation of getting off-hours work emails, and the constant checking for them, are spiking stress levels."

Luckily, there are solutions we can use today, and we can use technology in our favor. The Better Work Toolkit did not anticipate the massive shift to virtual/hybrid work during the pandemic. However, this toolkit does offer simple and practical solutions for managing flexible time in a prepandemic cult of busyness:

- Create slack. Put daily or weekly time in your calendar to account for unanticipated shocks and planning fallacy bias.
- Make it costly to send business emails after hours. Use technology to schedule emails to go out during the workday. Or design a prompt that asks someone to think twice before hitting send.
- Create autoresponders for off-hour email. Signaling email sent outside of work hours helps create a new norm. Taking time off to rest and reenergize is more valued than burning out.
- Make refreshing the inbox a conscious choice. Removing auto refresh disrupts the cycle of constant checking and interruption.

- Use commitment devices. Colleagues, teams, and organizations can use precommitment strategies to help meet deadlines, cut meeting time, or leave the office or stop working at a certain hour.

Prepandemic thought leadership and tools like The Better Work Toolkit remain illustrative and helpful. However, *we are ready for more*. The pandemic forced a massive two-year experiment in virtual/hybrid work, which has accelerated trends that were already happening at work—trends where technology became overwhelming. We were already feeling like our technology owned our time, rather than being helper robots which helped us create more time for leisure, play, and rest.

PUTTING ROBOTS IN THEIR PLACE

I confess for many years I hated iPhones. Being fairly obsessed with time management and getting things done (see my examples above), I loved PalmPilots. It was a digital organizer device first released in 1997 with simple robot functions: a digital calendar, a digital to-do-list, and a digital phone book.

My PalmPilot felt like the future. It fit in the large pocket of my medical student white coat. It felt like a small robot helper. It didn't beep at me, flash, or tempt me to play games. It served me and kept things organized—that's it. I loved my PalmPilot and continued to purchase the new versions, which got smaller and slightly fancier over time.

Late to get a cell phone, I finally got a fancy Sony square with a little flip-down mouthpiece. This phone did one thing—make phone calls. It was not smart, and I continued to use my handy PalmPilot as my main robot helper. When I finally got a shiny new iPhone in 2012, I was lazy. I didn't bother to learn how to use it properly. I would download apps without setting the configurations or notifications. It beeped and buzzed and generally annoyed me for years. I felt like I had to have it with me at all times in case an urgent phone call from the kids' school might arrive.

In 2018, things got ridiculous. I had almost one hundred apps in no particular order on the phone, notifications popping up at the worst times, and I got all kinds of spam announcements and phone calls. Ironically, I pride myself in being tech-savvy, as evidenced by my super-cool PalmPilot, so this laziness had nothing to do with the ability to figure out the smartphone. In my mindset, the smartphone existed to serve me. I was frustrated that my iPhone did not help me. It behaved like my master.

I have since learned all the phone configurations and continue to pay attention to feature updates. I routinely get rid of apps or move them around. I set focus times so I would not be disturbed. I turn off notifications and block spam callers. I even started using an Apple Watch so I could get important phone and text messages from the kids' school without having the smartphone nearby. This constant monitoring of my device takes time and energy.

Despite my newfound iPhone savvy, I have a love/hate relationship with my little iPhone robot. At times, it helps me perfectly, guiding me somewhere on a map or quickly looking up a fact I have forgotten. At other times, it still behaves like my master. It beeps and buzzes when I do not want it to, it wants me to spend endless amounts of time verifying my identification and updating my passwords. I know tech can be better, and I want to feel like I did when I had my PalmPilot—I have a super helpful little robot in my pocket—and it does not try to own me or my time.

Happily, there are technology leaders and designers who see a better way. One example of a technology product shaping itself around real humans is the online collaboration tool called Miro (Miro 2022). The CEO of Miro, Andrey Khusid, explicitly designed a tech tool that acts as a robot helper rather than a master.

Andrey grew up in the Netherlands. He has a rich background in design, winning several design competitions in his youth. Inheriting an entrepreneurial spirit he learned from his father, Andrey ran a creative agency called Vitamin Group from 2005–2012. In 2011, he founded Miro to bring his innovative design approach into the world of technology, with the idea a blank canvas can solve many problems. He originally designed Miro as a virtual whiteboard for design and product teams to work because at his own design firm he found a huge problem communicating with his remote clients.

When I use Miro with my teams, it feels different. I can organize my work in a way that is visual and evolves over time. I share my Miro boards with my team, and our interaction is visible. We work together synchronously and asynchronously in the same workspace. The boards are infinite, so we can see how the work is progressing over time. If we want to add fun, there are features like icebreakers, emojis, and stickers. If we need to make a decision, we use the voting tool.

This technology tool feels different because a designer rather than a business person created it. It was created by people who work with their hands to create objects, not by business people sitting in cubicles in the traditional office. This tool feels like it was designed for real human beings.

Miro helped me do my work more efficiently and better manage my time. I am blissfully unaware of all the thought, effort, and technological expertise which goes into this feeling for me as a user. Happily, people like Andrey are doing the hard work of understanding how real human beings work. The Miro designers understand the uses of technology to make humans feel more efficient, less overwhelmed, better able to communicate with virtual teams, and in more control of our time.

At the virtual 2021 Miro Distributed Conference, Andrey gave a keynote speech explaining his philosophy (Miro 2022). He said:

"We have an opportunity to make a difference by bringing more joy and more connection to people through software with Miro. Members of a team can express themselves differently depending on what makes them comfortable. Miro is still software, but it's a fun software. I think that's a pretty big thing for a global community full of people who want to continue expressing themselves, continue to be who they are, and continue to connect and learn from each other. We're not just helping people connect. We're helping them to be who they are and enjoy being together in a way they've been missing."

The connection between self-expression and fun is brilliant. *Helper robots like Miro should help us have more fun at work.*

"We want Miro to be an extension of your brain. You should be able to dump everything in Miro and then work through it with other brains on your team. Our job is to help and structure everything in a way that allows you to share it with other people, collaborate, and build on top of each other and eventually get to this point of mutual understanding. We want you to feel that your team is aligned and that you were able to get through a difficult task together. That's a great emotional moment for your team, but it's also a productive moment that moves your work forward," he said.

Highlighting the emotional connection between human beings is another reason Miro works. *New tech tools for work become great when they facilitate human emotions.* Work teams have strong bonds when they connect emotionally.

"I think there's a real opportunity to find ways for people to connect in the way that works best for them. That's how we're going to bring people together and help them feel more connected. We can make sure the best ideas rise to the top and help everyone move forward," he said.

In section III of this book, I will discuss human connectedness in more depth. When we select our tech tools, we can choose tools that promote connectedness. Miro is only one example of this type of tool. Rather than focusing on which tools are the best, we should focus on what the tools accomplish for their human clients.

SUMMARY

For the past century, most Americans have increasingly become part of a cult of busyness. Without being aware of it, we are sacrificing leisure and rest time for the status symbol of busyness. As technology tools at work increased, rather than becoming more efficient and having increased leisure and rest time, we have allowed endless to-do lists and poor boundaries between work and leisure to suck us in.

Many of our attempts to self-regulate and manage our time fail because of common psychological traps. As human beings, we are sloppy with our time, and we overcommit. As a member of the cult of busyness, saying yes to too many tasks makes us feel good because we are generating more busyness.

To let our brains play and rest, we must aggressively reclaim our time. In this aim, technology can be a friend or foe. There are tech leaders creating tools designed for human beings to make robot helpers, which allow us to reclaim our time and energy. Miro is an example of a technology tool that promotes human traits like self-expression, emotional connectedness, and fun.

Being aware of your own human tendencies to fall prey to the cult of busyness, your own psychological traps, and misbehaving technology—you can take steps to regain control over your time. This is a foundational step to making work not suck, but it is not the only step. The next section of this book will focus on communication and how you can understand your current communication patterns at work, strategies to improve your communication, and tactics to make small changes today.

CHAPTER 5

Asynchronous Communication

—

Prepandemic, our work communication shifted to more and more digital text, and email fatigue was a daily reality. During COVID-19, most of us incorporated more direct messaging tools into our workflows, and we were completely overwhelmed.

Bad news—written text communication overload causes fatigue and miscommunication and is a huge waste of time.

Good news—intentional communication planning saves time and energy and makes chatting fun again.

START SMALL—HIEROGLYPHICS WERE AN ANCIENT EGYPT VERSION OF EMOJIS

When you think of all the types of communication you use at work, it can be overwhelming. Before jumping into all the kinds of communication and how you can use them effectively at work, let's break it down into categories: symbols/emojis, text/DM/IM, and email.

Thinking small, the smallest form of asynchronous communication is the emoji. Emojis are symbols that express emotion or meaning without letters or text. The first and most well-known emoji is the smiley face from 1982 (Bellis 2019).

How, why, and when to use emojis confused me for many years. I finally understood in 2021 when I took an online course through my alma mater Penn focusing on ancient Egypt (Coursera 2022; The University of Pennsylvania 2022). Penn has a long history of archeological digs in Egypt, and its museum has an extraordinary collection of Egyptian artifacts. I have fond memories of taking an anthropology class at the Penn museum as an undergraduate and the sense of awe I experienced when I entered the building (Penn museum 2022).

In today's workplace, we find ourselves relying more and more on asynchronous digital communication tools like messaging, texting, and email. One challenge we face in communicating digitally is tone. One suggestion: use emojis to express tone. You can thereby avoid miscommunication, confusion, and anxiety. For example, when responding with a text "okay," you could also send an emoji for a happy face, a sad face, or a thumbs-up symbol. Notice the difference in tone for your "okay" when you use these different emojis.

In ancient Egypt, hieroglyphs correlated to consonant sounds. However, this did not include vowels. Therefore, confusion could arise when multiple words have the same consonants and different vowels. To remedy this confusion, they would add a *determinative* symbol at the end of the word to indicate the word's meaning. An example of a determinative would be adding an image of a boat to the word *sl* to indicate the word *sail* rather than *sale* or *sell*. I had an a-ha moment—emojis are like determinatives!

After taking this course on ancient Egypt, I saw emojis in a new light. Rather than a fun distraction or replacement for words, emojis are a different kind of **nonverbal communication**. This got me curious, why have emojis become so popular as a form of nonverbal communication in the digital age?

It turns out human brains love emojis because they are shorthand for emotions. As humans, we are excellent at reading facial muscle movements as a proxy for emotion. Each culture is slightly different. We appear hardwired to understand the correlation between our primary emotions and our facial expression (Matsumoto 2011).

According to a 2014 study published in the journal *Social Neuroscience*, looking at simple emojis—faces crafted from colons and parentheses—can trigger the same facial recognition response in the occipitotemporal parts of the brain. Gazing at other human facial expressions triggers the same pattern of brain activation (Churches 2014).

In other words, looking at a *real* face, a picture of a face, or an emoji all have the same brain activation pattern.

Since our brains love emojis—and they can quickly and easily communicate tone, emotion, and intention in a nonverbal manner—emojis are an effective digital communication tool.

An emoji can be the perfect tool to connect with someone quickly, using minimal effort and the highest level of accuracy possible. Adding a checkbox symbol to a text indicates you have read the text rather than writing out, "I have read this." Adding a thumb-up symbol to a yes or no question can mean, "Yes, I agree." Once you get used to reading and using emojis, your communication is quicker, more effective, and *makes your brain feel better* than relying on text only.

USING SYMBOLS TO BUILD CULTURE AT WORK

Emojis are the smallest form of communication because they directly activate our brain cells for facial expression. The next layer of communication is symbolic. Before humans wrote words, they communicated with symbols. In modern times, children understand symbols years before they communicate through reading and writing. In addition to emojis, other types of symbols enhance communication at work.

Prepandemic, I was highly skeptical of using symbols to communicate within a work setting. After understanding why our brains feel *good* looking at emojis and experimenting with personal texts, I changed my mind. I decided to use emojis and symbols in my workplace to work smarter with my virtual teams.

In spring 2021, I consulted with a healthcare start-up to build the company from scratch. An anchor client was ready to start work with them in January 2022, so the pressure was on to build the company quickly and hire forty people before the end of the year. In the beginning, communication was simple. We used our personal emails, cell phones, and video calls.

As the next three to five people came on board, we had the opportunity to take a moment and ask, "What communication do we want to build?" One of the things I love most about this company is the idea that we can challenge all assumptions and build something totally new. So, I thought of all the communication styles I had seen in the past and the trauma of walking into work with 400 emails sitting on my desk. I swore that would never happen to me again!

We decided to use Slack as our primary daily communication tool (Slack 2022). At first, I found the DM system and the Slack interface quite awkward. Over time, I watched what other people were doing in Slack, asked questions of my younger colleagues, and tried different strategies. After three months, we found a way to use Slack with DM and emojis, which was highly effective and efficient. We continue to refine how we communicate as the team grows from a handful of people to an anticipated one hundred people by the end of the year.

One of my favorite ways we used symbols was to create a symbol for each of the company's core values. Then, whenever we saw someone demonstrating a value in Slack, we selected the symbol for the core value and added it to our comments. Over time, we used these customized symbols in a variety of communication platforms—on slide decks, on collaborative whiteboards, and on marketing materials. The more these core values symbols sank into the culture of the organization, the more the core values sank into our default mindset. The combination of words and symbols became a key part of our strategy to build and retain strong teams, leading to better outcomes at work.

THE PERILS OF EMAIL

While emojis and symbols are small and often underutilized communication tools, they only convey a small amount of daily communication. Before we discuss chat/DM/IM, let's jump ahead and take a closer look at email. Email has become a villainous character in work and home life for many people, and for good reason.

Many leaders search for the *watercooler* in virtual work. In the traditional office, the watercooler hosted informal, quick, creative conversations. While organizations have been using chatting platforms like Slack or Microsoft Teams, many organizations still rely on email to communicate everything.

Originally designed to replace paper mail and memos, the first email was sent in 1971. Academics and researchers designed email to communicate with one another (*The Guardian* 2016). Since then, email has continued to show explosive growth. As of 2022, there are approximately 333.2 billion emails sent per day (Ceci 2022). The speed of opening emails has also increased, and one paper found that 50 percent of responses are sent within two hours, and the most common email response time is two minutes (Blumenthal 2015). Given this accelerated pace, many people continue to use email as a default place to chat, get quick responses, and ask questions that need a quick answer. Not surprisingly, statistics show the average person gets over one hundred emails a day (not counting spam) and the average working professional sends at least forty emails per day (Wise 2022).

Email is fraught with perils because using high-volume, quick response time, text-only, one-to-one communication *makes tone extraordinarily difficult.* During the pandemic, I participated in a fascinating online workshop where Erica Dhawan discussed key concepts on how to communicate in the virtual workspace. Erica is a thought leader in twenty-first-century teamwork. She concluded most of us are not equipped to understand **digital body language** (Dhawan 2021).

What is digital body language? Digital body language is body language invisible at first glance, which you use in the digital space when you communicate via email, messenger, chat, or conference call. The way in which you communicate digitally reflects you, your attitude, your intentions, and your expectations. Each new form of communication has its own body language without a codified norm to guide us. So, all day we struggle to understand not only words and images but also the underlying message in the digital body language in front of us. Digital body language exhausts our human brains because we are still not practiced, and the norms are often vague or missing altogether.

We all struggle with email because each group has its own social norms around email. One group might use it to chat, expecting a response in sixty seconds between the hours of 8 a.m. and 5 p.m. Another group might use email only for long memo-style, preferring phone calls or meetings to catch up.

A third group might use email to communicate team updates and rely on in-person work to plan and make decisions. As a leader, a manager, or an employee, *we are all trying to figure out the hidden body language of email without explicitly stating and upholding the group's expectations.*

So what's next? Team leaders must intentionally set norms for the different forms of communication, and teams must practice these norms daily. To minimize digital body language anxiety, Erica Dhawan created a variety of psychologically savvy tips (Dhawan 2021). For example, she said:

"[When using] email, avoid anxiety-inducing subject lines like 'Please call me.' They're the workplace equivalent of 'we need to talk' and are never necessary. This is not what we mean by 'action-oriented.' Brief does not mean lacking context."

This tip doesn't tell the whole story. *Email is only one form of asynchronous communication*—perhaps the most loved and hated. Almost everyone has a strong reaction to using email—good or bad. For example, I recently attended a team meeting where one team member shared that email makes them feel safe and secure, whereas another team member felt traumatized by email. I, too, have experienced anxiety spiraling out of control as a result of email—have you?

Commercial email has existed since the 1990s, and almost everyone has their own email nightmare anxiety story. Six months into the pandemic, I worked at home as a healthcare executive, and I had a new boss. The new boss started during the pandemic. I did not meet him in person. He had a variety of anxiety-inducing communication habits. His communications were infrequent and curt, and he did not offer feedback unless under duress.

I sat in my home office, the autumn light spilling in through the window, and I peacefully viewed my laptop with a cup of coffee. I opened my email and saw a message: *"Please call me."* No context and no hint of the topic. I waited until 9 a.m. and called my boss. No answer. I waited. As three cups of coffee poured into my blood, I felt the first tinges of anxiety. I called again at 10 a.m., nothing. Now what? Should I keep calling? Respond to the email? Wait?

The morning proceeded, and I was worried. What happened? Did I make an error? Was the boss angry? I called again at 11 a.m. and noon, nothing. I sent a text. Nothing. After lunch, my anxiety rose higher and higher. Another call with no answer. No answer to my text. Eventually, at the end of the day, around 4 p.m. I sent an email "I have been trying to call but haven't heard back."

I spent the evening in a state of anxiety. In the morning, around 8 a.m., the boss finally called me. He said:

"Did you complete the PTO form for your team? We need to have it turned in today, so I am checking with everyone."

My head exploded. I completed the form days ago, the same way I did every two weeks. He didn't even check online to see if I had completed the form.

In this example, my boss and I did not have a conversation concerning the use of email, his expectations, and my expectations. As a result, our email body language was confusing and led to a massive emotional communication breakdown. There has to be a better way to chat and have quick and meaningful conversations in the virtual workspace. Email is a terrible virtual watercooler.

A BETTER WAY TO CHAT

At this point, many of you may be thinking—email obviously sucks. You also know emojis and symbols are not enough to communicate with your team. So now what?

Given that email is a poor substrate for quick virtual communication, there must be a better way for quick chats and questions. Chat/IM/DM tools are rapidly becoming a preferred method for asynchronous communication within teams. We are still learning ways to best use chat/IM/DM, and people of different generations may use these tools differently.

Recently, I sat down with Kate Snyder, who works as a senior consultant in HR Technology at an international financial organization of over 17,000 employees. Kate is a calm and collected woman and a great listener.

As someone on the cusp of two generations: GenX and millennials, Kate is interested in how different generations function in the current workplace. Curious to get Kate's understanding of how digital body language has changed during the pandemic, I asked how she has seen this play out amongst different generations at her organization. I asked Kate what she has seen in terms of digital body language pre and post-pandemic, and what worked well. She said:

"From a tools perspective, prepandemic, all generations prior to the millennials would prefer emails, but the millennials don't want to read emails. Because of the pandemic, I feel like people across all generations have gotten better at using the tools that are available to them."

She described how the pandemic forced workers at her company to switch over to Microsoft Teams from email and in-person informal conversations. Before the shift, younger workers tended to use IM, and older workers tended to use email and phone calls. The pandemic shift forced a new social norm, and everyone used the same IM tools. As a result, she saw improvement in the speed of getting things done and making decisions.

Kate shared an example from her work when she led an implementation team with frequent questions, tweaks, and quick decisions. She said:

"My team is responsible for supporting implementations, so we supported a release of a new application across the organization. We knew there would be many questions, but after the launch, we quickly realized an unanticipated problem.

"In the previous world, we would have sent out an email and tried to get everybody in the room together by scheduling a formal meeting. Instead, I was able to send a team's chat to four different people and say, 'Hey, guys, you know, I know this is last minute. We discovered this issue—can we pull together today for fifteen minutes to talk through what the solution might be?' We would have never been able to do this before in our previous system."

During our conversation, Kate also told me that using IM/DM/chats has led older generations to be much more agile, more willing to move quickly, and to brainstorm together. As a result, Kate has seen her business unit move much more quickly.

Kate also has seen her multigenerational teams make decisions much more quickly using chat. In the past, the older colleagues would schedule a meeting and spend time before the meeting doing fact-finding. The meeting preparation time ended up being counterproductive. People would arrive to the meeting with fixed notions of the solution, and it would be difficult to have a more open-ended brainstorming session.

Kate said, "Chat-based decision-making process succeeds across generations, and it levels the playing field so that everyone can work together to find a solution."

Why did this chat-based decision-making process move faster in the remote setting as opposed to the in-person setting? *It seemed counterintuitive that a group could make a decision faster in the remote setting.*

Kate shared her best practices for using IM to make a decision in the virtual setting.

First, she messages everyone on one chat, saying, "Hey, I'm messaging you because of X. Do you guys have a minute if I call you in?" If everybody's available, she will open audio on the chat application for a conversation.

Second, if they're unavailable and won't be available quickly, Kate puts the question in the chat itself.

"People respond whenever they have time, and they'll build off each other's responses. If there is a clear decision point, then after the fact, we would get everybody together to formalize the decision point."

"Often an official decision point isn't even needed because on the chat, they can give a thumbs-up to show they approve the decision," she said.

Kate sees people are comfortable with this type of asynchronous decision-making because the text is tracked, creating a paper trail they can use as an artifact. It surprised her at first, but she sees it as a valuable tool to speed up decision-making in the virtual setting. I was also surprised—decisions without meetings—mastering this skill could massively impact the speed and agility of virtual work.

MAKING ASYNCHRONOUS WORK SMARTER

Why should we bother to change the way we are currently working? Why does asynchronous work matter?

Communication overload plagued the American workplace. Even before the pandemic, email inboxes exploded, the workday stretched into the evening and weekend, and we pondered *work-life balance*. Mental health problems and substance use disorders rose and grabbed the news headlines.

As a result of the pandemic, for many people, *communication overload became much, much worse.* We find ourselves pinged around the clock with the rise of multiple forms of asynchronous communication (email, IM/DM, Slack, Teams, text). We feel overworked and overwhelmed on a daily basis. Rather than try to fix the problem, many leaders and managers stubbornly continue to try to go back to normal, but there is a new normal. Ignoring mental health and work/life flexibility is no longer an option. *The Great Resignation* of 2021 demonstrated the talent in our workforce, especially in younger generations, are no longer willing to put up with work which makes us miserable (Parker 2022).

Businesses that do not adapt and embrace new ways of working asynchronously bear risk. They risk losing talent. They risk being slow and inefficient. They risk having a workplace that sucks.

As an optimist, I am fascinated by how virtual work forces us to change the way we communicate asynchronously. The social rules of virtual communication are changing. New virtual work tools have made it possible to reimagine how we work together, and we have new opportunities for more effectiveness and efficiency. I particularly enjoy learning how to use new virtual work tools to bring people together in new ways. Generations who were disconnected have the opportunity to connect. People in different time zones, different countries, and different continents have the opportunity to work together. We face both great opportunity as well as great uncertainty.

We are all pioneering in this new workspace together, so having a sense of humor helps, and assuming good intent is critical (see Part III on empathy). If I make a mistake and use the wrong emoji or don't use the IM properly, or misinterpret someone else's communication, I take the time to say something like this:

"I made a mistake—this is what I meant to communicate. I guess we are all still figuring out this virtual communication. Thanks for your understanding and patience."

Part IV of this book discusses the future of asynchronous work. We can make small changes today, which will significantly improve our experience of asynchronous work and lay the foundation for the future.

CHAPTER 6

Synchronous Communication

———

Think back to your last virtual meeting.

- Were you bored? Tired? Confused?
- Did the leader of the meeting engage your attention throughout?
- Did you leave the meeting feeling a connection with others in the virtual room?
- Did you leave the meeting with a clear sense of purpose and inspiration?

In virtual work, synchronous communication becomes performance—we must practice how to perform in this new setting. Important techniques to master are storytelling and emotional impact. Using these skills kills Zoom fatigue and makes virtual meetings shorter and more effective.

COMMUNICATION BREAKDOWN

On a hot Sunday afternoon in August 1992, weeks shy of my nineteenth birthday, I landed at Paris Charles de Gaulle Airport with a one hundred-pound duffle bag and rudimentary French language skills. My ride, an unreliable friend-of-a-friend, failed to show up at the airport. Tired, hungry, excited, and scared, I had to navigate my way to a hostel in Paris, eat, shower, and prepare to show up at my first class in the morning across town.

I remember this day well because I suffered a variety of communication breakdowns. Without Google Translator or smartphones, there was plenty of room for disaster. I miscommunicated with my ride and had no way to reach them. With limited French, I navigated myself and my giant duffel bag through the subways of Paris.

Sweaty and worried, I eventually arrived at the hostel and took a glorious shower. Hungry, I searched for food. Little did I know in the outskirts of Paris, all the restaurants and the hostel cafeteria were closed on Sunday. I searched for a deli or a vending machine with food. Nope. I totally missed the French cultural memo—everything was closed on Sunday. French people typically did not snack, so there were no delis or vending machines.

Another student at the hostel had pity and gave me bread and cheese. After another round of navigating the subway, I arrived at my school the next day and was completely confused all over again. The teachers were speaking 100 percent in French, and expectations differed. It took six months before I communicated effectively. While I expected verbal communication to take time to learn, I grossly underestimated the time it took to communicate culturally and how the intersection of verbal and cultural communication played out.

When the pandemic hit in early 2020, and many people started working virtually, most of us immediately experienced a communication breakdown. As of the writing of this book, several years have passed, and many people still feel disoriented.

One of the biggest complaints I heard in the last few years was the fatigue caused by video meetings. In an effort to recreate communication in a physical office, many organizations switched over to video meetings back-to-back all day long.

As time progressed and the immediate crisis of the pandemic wore on, people started discussing Zoom fatigue. Nonstop video communication exhausted us. In 2021, researchers took a closer look—why did videoconferencing cause so much distress and fatigue? Professor Jeffrey Bailensen of the Stanford Virtual Human Interaction Lab published an article that deconstructed video fatigue from a psychological perspective (Bailenson 2021).

The Stanford lab designed a fifteen-item questionnaire, which asks questions about a person's general fatigue, physical fatigue, social fatigue, emotional fatigue, and motivational fatigue. Using this Zoom Exhaustion and Fatigue Scale, researchers found four primary reasons for video fatigue (VHIL 2022):

1. Excessive amounts of close-up eye contact is intense
2. Seeing yourself constantly in video chats in real time is exhausting

3. Video chats dramatically reduce our physical mobility
4. The cognitive load, the amount of work your brain has to do, is much higher in video chats

If you think about this from a brain and behavior perspective, it makes complete sense. You may remember from the introduction that humans have both face cells and mirror cells in the brain. Excessive and abnormal activation of these neurons increases the load on brain functioning and causes us to tire.

On the third point, sitting in front of a computer all day long exhausts us because our bodies are not in motion. Even prepandemic, everyone experienced frustration with being tied to a little box on our desk. In the physical office setting, we stood up to go to the bathroom and stretch our legs. So why did many people start doing back-to-back video meetings with no breaks?

I believe the answer is simple—we default to thirty- and sixty-minute increment meetings because most calendars default to those increments of time. Behavioral scientists researched the power of defaults and how they are powerful tools to subconsciously affect human behavior (Jachimowica 2019). A good example of defaults is 401(k) enrollment. A 2021 Vanguard study showed when companies make 401(k) enrollment, the default—new hire 401(k) enrollment dramatically increases from 91 percent under automatic enrollment compared with 28 percent under voluntary enrollment (Vanguard 2021).

Look at your online calendar—when you make a meeting or appointment, does it default to sixty minutes? Systems are starting to offer different defaults of twenty or forty-five minutes. In fact, it is easy to set up tech, so shorter meetings are the default when you use an online calendar system. Of course, it still takes habit building for human behavior to shorten meeting times. Having a set default is helpful. Leaders and managers have the ability to set the standard for their teams and model shorter meetings with breaks.

So, imagine a virtual workspace where you optimized the use of video calls, shortened meeting times, and added breaks. Maybe you feel less fatigued and have more physical movement in your day. Why do your synchronous meetings still suck?

Most synchronous virtual meetings use PowerPoint or other visual tools to share data and information. People pack slides full of facts and figures in an attempt to add value to the meeting, and before you know it, they are reading off their slides. The meeting sucks. As visual presentation tools have become easier to use, many people have forgotten the power of storytelling. Understanding storytelling leads to better presentations and better meetings.

WHY HUMANS LOVE STORIES

In a (prepandemic) 2020 TEDx Talk, Karen Eber explained how the most effective leaders use a combination of storytelling and data. She also described the neuroscience underlying this effect (Eber 2022).

"Storytelling and data are actually not this either-or. It's an *and*, they actually create this power ballad that connects you to information differently," she said.

Karen described how when you are in a meeting and the presenter shows data—numbers, statistics—two small parts of your brain are activated. These areas process speech and are called Wernicke's (speech comprehension) and Broca's (speech motor) areas. This type of information is easy to forget because it is only based on words and numbers.

On the other hand, when you listen to a story, your senses and your emotions engage. Your entire brain lights up. When a presenter tells a story of a phone falling and hitting the ground with a thud, your brain lights up in the areas connected to seeing a phone fall (occipital lobe) and hearing the phone thud on the ground (temporal lobe). Karen describes this phenomenon as **neural coupling.** As a story is told, the brain of the storyteller lights up exactly like the brain of the listener. In this example, both brains light up as if the storyteller and the listener actually experience the phone falling to the ground.

Explaining why both storytelling and data presentations are needed for listeners to retain information, Karen said:

"First—data doesn't change our behavior; emotions do. If data changed our behavior, we would all sleep eight hours and exercise and floss daily and drink eight glasses of water. But that's not how we actually decide. Neuroscientists have studied decision-making, and it starts in our amygdala. This area centers our emotional experience, and it's here at a subconscious level where we begin to decide. We make choices to pursue pleasure or to avoid risk, all before we become aware of it. At the point we become aware, where it comes to the conscious level, we start to apply rationalization and logic. Consciously, we think we're making these rationally based decisions, not realizing our subconscious has already decided.

"Second—data never speaks for itself. Our brains love to anticipate and as we anticipate, we fill in the gaps in what we're seeing or hearing with our own knowledge and experience and our own bias. Which means my understanding of data is going to differ from yours, and it's going to differ from yours because we're all going to have our own interpretation if there isn't a way to guide us through."

Karen concluded that *using both data and storytelling in a harmonious fashion is the best way to engage the listener.* You can achieve harmony by telling a story of the data itself. Another tactic is for the presenter to tell a parallel story, highlighting points from the story to reinforce the data.

I experienced the power of storytelling firsthand when my national team of behavioral health clinicians switched to virtual work at the beginning of the pandemic. At the time, our story was—we were pioneers in this new world of virtual health, and we would be learning together and looking at both subjective and objective data to guide our practice.

Over the past few years, I successfully reduced the number of my daily video meetings. However, I continued to struggle to make the most of synchronous time. I, too, fell into the trap of cramming a bunch of data, images, or subjective comments into a synchronous video meeting. I wondered how I could improve my own skills to weave together data and storytelling.

One of the reasons I decided to write this book was the opportunity to learn from Eric Koester and the Creator Institute how to tell stories (Creator Institute 2022). What have I learned so far? Storytelling is both more complicated and more simple than I anticipated. There are familiar patterns of stories that help humans communicate. It is easy to formulate and learn these patterns (for example, see *The Seven Basic Plots* book (Booker 2019)). However, becoming a better storyteller requires the author to prepare, practice, and iterate based on the response of the audience.

When storytelling through writing, you are limited to the words on the page. One of the most promising parts of working virtually is the ability to bring in more visual and auditory material—like videos, music, icons, and animations. I believe this is *an advantage for virtual work because it can facilitate making an emotional connection with the audience.*

EMOTIONS BIND US TOGETHER

Although often ignored in the workplace, emotions are a powerful part of being human, and emotions play a powerful role in how teams function. In my work over the years, I have been fascinated by seeing groups of highly intelligent, rational professionals struggle with making change. *It is often the invisible, unconscious, emotional component of the change that makes the difference between success and failure.*

Chip and Dan Heath discussed this phenomenon in their book *Switch*, which described the techniques needed to work with human psychology to make a change in organizations (Heath 2010).

They used the metaphor of an elephant and a Rider, where the elephant symbolizes a person's subconscious, emotional side, and the Rider is the conscious, rational side. They argued that when change works, it's because leaders are speaking to the elephant as well as the Rider.

They described how leaders often fall into the trap of providing rational, data-driven, articulate arguments, as well as thoughtful, effective operational systems to make change.

They said, "Because of the uncertainty that change brings, the elephant is reluctant to move, and analytical arguments will not overcome that reluctance."

In other words, *to get human beings to take action, you must help them see and feel the action you want them to take.* In the world of virtual work, common best practices of sharing facts and figures, setting up solid operations, and explaining the goals rationally are not enough. Leaders and managers must find ways to bring the emotional component to the table at team synchronous meetings.

Connecting back to the Why or the mission of the group adds emotional impact to synchronous meetings. Showing powerful images or videos elicits emotion, including humor. *Discussing pain points and painting a picture of what a better future holds helps teams rally.*

PRACTICING TO PERFORM

When I thought of people who successfully use emotional impact in their synchronous communication, I immediately thought of my friend and colleague, Dr. Ellen Walker. A psychiatrist and psychotherapist by training, Dr. Ellen is also a talented pianist. In September 2020, Dr. Ellen moved to Northern California from Utah, and started a new position as a physician leader and psychiatric consultant in a 100 percent remote setting. As with many healthcare leaders during the pandemic, she found herself leading a team of mental health providers across the country who themselves had never worked remotely before.

I asked Dr. Ellen about her experience with virtual work. She reflected on how she learned how to communicate meaningfully in the remote setting through her experiences performing piano.

She said, "To get to a high-performance level, there has to be enough time and self-care to be able to relax and to perform creatively because that's the way our mind works the best. I know it sounds super basic, but I notice that when stress gets too high, it inhibits performance.

"What I have learned through playing piano is that, however much I practice the music itself, I also need to practice performing for other people and putting myself in that environment. I'm not a huge fan of performing. Part of that is because, in my heart, I'm shy and I don't like to be on stage.

"For example, I learned a piece of music for four months, and I performed it after being on a hiatus from performing for a few years. I had no memory of what performance felt like. I went into this performance, and I guess you could say it went well enough, but I was totally in fight or flight, and I had memory slips. This is not normally a problem for me because I memorize my music so I can then focus on interpretation.

"When I went back to my music teacher after this performance, he told me to practice performing. Week one, he said, get out your stuffed animals and perform for them. Week two, play in front of friends. Continue to play in front of larger groups of people and people who know the music—you cannot fake it with them.

"This idea of music performance is so helpful for me at my current job because I've been called on to give several presentations, and it is like being on stage. I have to think quickly with questions. It feels like a performance because I have to make it fun. Otherwise, the topic becomes boring.

"I tell myself before a presentation that I am talking with an audience. This is a show, and I need to engage my audience. I realized that you're having a conversation, whether it's music or a work presentation. Now I go into presentations thinking: this is what I want to express, and I really focus on trying to give that to the audience rather than focusing on the notes (for music) or the content (for work)."

I related to Dr. Ellen's story in two ways.

First, I love the idea of *over practicing the content of your work presentation so it is second nature.* When you are early in your career, work presentations require repetition and diligence to solidify in the neuronal net in your brain. In medical school, we frequently drilled on the same facts over and over again. Our professors added an emotional component—they embarrassed us when we did not know our facts. Later in your career, you mastered the facts, so it took less time and effort to be over practiced—the brain network became solid.

Second, I love the idea of *performance at work is a conversation*, in the same way music performance is a communication with the audience. Sometimes the content (or notes) are less important than the idea or feeling conveyed to the audience. You can have a perfect performance; however, if the audience takes nothing away or doesn't feel anything during the performance, you have failed at having the conversation.

So how can we take these ideas into the workplace of the future?

Communication requires both content and performance. For each communication, we can ask ourselves the following questions:

- What is the content I am trying to communicate?
- Who is my audience?
- Where is my audience likely coming from? What is their mental model coming into my communication?
- What is the feeling I want my audience to have after my communication?
- How can I make it fun or interesting?
- What can I do during my communication to make it more likely for them to take away something meaningful?

Practicing performance requires extra time and energy—we invest in your work relationships and your own professional development. If you are shy, introverted, or someone who did not grow up making your voice heard, you will have to learn to perform. When we start performing, we will feel the adrenaline response kick in, and we can use the concept of **exposure therapy** to help. Dr. Ellen's music teacher explained to her how to use Exposure Therapy to get more comfortable performing. First, she performed in front of stuffed animals, then she worked her way up to friends, until she could play in front of large groups of strangers.

In the virtual work setting, performance happens in video presentations. Dr. Ellen has worked virtually for two years and shared her insights into virtual performance.

"I think people who work remotely have to work harder to connect with their audience. So, if that means making it a little more laid back and conversational, injecting humor, or whatever works best with your personality. So, I guess it means taking the time to know yourself well enough to know what feels comfortable and then practicing that. Similar to psychotherapy, some people find comfort in remote presenting since there is more distance, and so they feel more able to open up. But other people find it a real barrier and seem more stilted. The latter group needs to work harder to overcome that resistance." she said.

Before preparing for a video presentation, we can take a little time to understand our personal style on video. If new to video without knowing what works or doesn't work, we can ask for feedback from trusted friends or colleagues. Then, to practice, we can take the following steps:

- Practice your content until it is 100 percent solid in your brain.
- Identify your audience.
- Identify how you want your audience to feel during your presentation and what you want them to walk away thinking and feeling.
- Write down three to five key audience goals on a sticky note.
- Practice giving your presentation out loud with sticky notes in front of you.
- Practice giving your presentation with your video recording and then watch it.
- Practice giving your presentation to a trusted friend or colleague and ask what they took away.
- Give yourself time and space to mentally and physically prepare the day of your presentation (i.e., do not book meetings right before the presentation, make sure your tech is working, put up your sticky note where you can see it, exercise, etc.).

This checklist leads to success for musicians, medical students, and successful work presenters. It takes time and repetition—the rewards are worth it. It also gets easier over time, and even shy people like Dr. Ellen can master presentations.

PUTTING IT ALL TOGETHER FOR SYNCHRONOUS VIR-TUAL WORK

If you are like me, you will celebrate the death of back-to-back video meetings filled with boring slide presentations and droning lectures. Using what we know of human brains and behavior, we can make synchronous virtual work shorter, more engaging, and more powerful.

CHAPTER 7

Subconscious Types of Communication

Our brains and bodies are closely connected. Just like when people are having success switching their video meetings to audio-only outside on a walk, tactics for successful work must consider both our thinking brain and our moving and sensing body.

In virtual work, we forget our subconscious brain and behavior. We understand concepts like verbal or nonverbal communication because we are typically able to focus our perception and attention to these concepts in a *thinking* way. Because we are able to observe them directly, we can take action to change how we communicate verbally and nonverbally.

However, a deeper dive into neuroscience tells us our brains are only part of our nervous system. Unconscious or subconscious processes within our brains and bodies drive the vast majority of our day-to-day existence. For example, as you read these words, your body works. Your heart beats regularly and adjusts its pace as needed. Your lungs breathe in air. Your gut digests food. Your immune system regulates your interior and exterior spaces. The list is endless, even when you are sleeping.

How do unconscious and subconscious bodily functions impact the way we work?

VIRTUAL REALITY AT WORK

Recently, I had my first virtual reality (VR) meeting. Admittedly, I was wary and skeptical. I don't typically enjoy video games, and past experiences trying VR gave me nausea. My work sent me a VR device free of charge, so there was nothing to lose.

Curious, I set up the device and synched it with my computer. I attended a meeting with Patrick Foley, the CEO of a healthcare start-up, and... it was really strange. My brain accepted the avatar version of Patrick. We sat together in a room. We moved to the virtual whiteboard together, and—strangely—we were occupying the same space. At the virtual whiteboard, our real-life heights matched, so I looked up a bit and he looked down a bit.

When I asked Patrick about his experience, he had a similar response—he said:

"It was like we were in the same room together. I really felt like I was in my office looking across the desk at you. When we went to the whiteboard together, I was struck by how real it felt. Somehow the VR even matched our heights to reality."

When I asked how it felt, he said: "There was a sense of presence. It added a layer of complexity."

Why on earth did our brains accept this?

In my experience, the VR worked (and why the VR I tried in the past didn't work) because the body language parts of the interface succeeded. I could *see* my virtual hands and see Patrick moving his mouth, his head, his body, and his hands more or less the way he did in the real world.

Traditional video platforms like Zoom do not have this rich body language. When you stare at the screen on Zoom, you have two choices:

- You can look at the camera so the other person feels you have eye contact with them
- You can look at the other person's eyes, so you feel you have eye contact with them.

You cannot have it both ways, so the eye contact on video is highly unnatural.

On video calls, below the level of the face, you cannot see any body language from the other person at all. Distorted eye contact without any other body language on video calls is also unnatural. It makes your brain go on alarm status. I found the VR meeting energizing rather than exhausting.

Even though I didn't love the weight of the device on my head, the pure fun of the experience surprised me.

This lends credence to the strange-but-true fact: *our perception of reality is a function that happens in our brain and is based on our sensations in our body and coming to us from the outside world via sensors.* The better VR gets at replicating this, the more we believe it.

In my VR call, we used avatars. The idea of a curated avatar interests me because you can have your best hair day every day, or if you are in a wild mood, you can dye your virtual hair purple for the meeting. It allows for forms of self-expression which could make interacting virtually easier and more fun.

After trying a VR meeting at work, I asked: *What are other uses of VR at work?*

USING VIRTUAL REALITY FOR DEEP WORK

Cal Newport is a computer science professor at Georgetown University and a best-selling author. Cal attributes much of his success to the idea of **deep work** (Newport 2016). He said:

"Professional activities performed in a state of distraction-free concentration push your cognitive capabilities to their limit. These efforts create new value, improve your skill, and are hard to replicate."

In his book on deep work, Cal gave examples of famous thinkers like Carl Jung and Mark Twain, who would shut themselves up in distraction-free rooms for long periods of time without interruption. He went on to show how for most professional workers today, deep work is rare, undervalued, and underutilized. Instead, we see **shallow work.**

Cal defined shallow work as noncognitive demanding, logistical-style tasks, often performed while distracted. These efforts tend not to create much new value in the world and are easy to replicate. Email, chats, and meetings are typical shallow work—sound familiar?

When did you last sit down for a 100 percent uninterrupted stretch of time to think at work? How long was it—fifteen minutes? An hour? A day? A week?

If efficient deep work creates high-value work and distracted shallow work creates low-value work, we should all be looking for ways to do more deep work. However, the old-fashioned tactic of putting yourself in a dusty university library or a cottage in the woods with no human or electronic contact for days and weeks on end is not a feasible option for most people.

In a 2021 New Yorker article, Cal acknowledged this problem and suggested virtual reality may be a solution (Newport 2021). He experimented with using a VR setting to create an environment for deep work using an inexpensive VR device and a productivity app. He describes the various feedback from the VR device—the way it feels to type, the sensory feedback from the virtual room. He said:

"All of this complexity must dovetail just right for me to forget, even if only for a few minutes, that I'm sitting on a worn chair in my office, next to a potted plant that I need to water and a desk cluttered with papers."

To me, it is 100 percent counterintuitive a digital virtual sensory environment leads to a higher quality of work. I would have imagined sitting in the VR chair at the VR desk in the VR office would feel wrong and foreign. I would have imagined the VR setting tempted the user to dash off and do fun things in their virtual environment.

The basis of my assumptions were on an older, slower, and clunkier version of commercially available VR. In a desire to gain market share and grab human attention spans, big tech companies have been investing in rapidly advancing VR. When I used VR for my meeting with Patrick, *I felt embodied—my thinking brain connected to my moving and sensing body—which made the difference for me.* Like Cal—I felt my body in the virtual space.

THE IMPORTANCE OF CONNECTING THE BRAIN AND BODY

Earlier, I discussed how we could learn how to play from an octopus. As I considered VR more deeply, I thought of the nervous system of the octopus again.

Did you know an octopus has multiple brains in each of its eight legs? The complex nervous system of the octopus has many small lobes in the central brain and a larger number of neurons located in its legs. This contrasts with the human brain with large complex lobes and a much smaller number of neurons in our bodies.

If you want to understand what it *feels* like to be an octopus, check out Sy Montgomery's book *The Soul of An Octopus* (Montgomery 2016). Sy described how the octopus uses its arms to multitask, taking in smells, tastes, and touches all at the same time. With vivid descriptions, he saw the personality, intelligence, and curiosity of each octopus. *This contrasts with how it feels to be human—an endless stream of thoughts and feelings paired with a limited sensory apparatus.*

Perhaps the octopus solves problems with ease due to a rich sensory apparatus and strongly embedded brain/body. *Humans are brain-heavy*—while the entire nervous system of an octopus has fifty million neurons (cells of the nervous system), human brains have an average of eighty-six billion neurons (University of Washington 2022).

Moreover, human brains are heavy on *thinking* modules. As compared to older parts of the brain (like the midbrain, hindbrain, cerebellum, and spinal cord), the human cerebral cortex makes up 77 percent by volume of the human nervous system. In contrast, the thinking cerebral cortex of the rat only makes up 31 percent by volume of the rat's nervous system.

Having so much brain available to think has obviously been highly adaptive to humans; however, a downside exists. *Humans can be so focused on their "thinking" brains—they disconnect from other parts of their nervous system, sometimes with disastrous consequences.*

As a psychiatrist, I worked with patients who had a profound disconnect between their thinking brains and their moving and sensing bodies. I saw intelligent, hard-working, thoughtful people being controlled entirely by unexplained symptoms in their bodies. A young woman suffered so greatly from emotional turmoil—her legs stopped working one day. A successful, middle-aged businessman suffered from confusing symptoms in his digestive tract, which rendered him completely nonfunctional at home and at work.

I used to believe thoughts and emotions of the brain controlled the rest of the body, and these patients had psychosomatic symptoms; i.e. their brain controlled their bodies. But it was more complicated. I worked with a young father with a strange neurological syndrome after a viral infection affected his ability to control his arms. His long interaction with the medical system traumatized him, and he suffered from severe anxiety, which persisted for years. I saw many patients who did not trust their gut, failing to escape dangerous situations. I saw patients with dramatic changes in their emotions and thought patterns after gaining or losing large amounts of weight—as if the fat cells were communicating with their brains.

So perhaps we humans are not as brain-dominant as we suppose. *Perhaps, like the octopus, our body has various complex nervous systems which can control our thoughts and emotions.* We know something in our hearts to be true. We have a gut feeling. Maybe we should take a closer look at our own multiple body-brains, the way the author searched for the soul of an octopus.

To stay mentally and physically healthy, humans need to keep their thinking brains and bodies connected. When the brain and body disconnect, human health suffers at home, at play, or at work. If you're thinking brain disconnects from your body at work, the quality of your work will also suffer.

HOW TO MANAGE OUR BRAINS AND BODIES AT WORK

You have likely heard of the negative consequences of looking at a screen all day. With our current technology, a 2021 article (Anderson 2021) reported:

- Most Americans spend more than seven hours a day staring at digital screens. Screens are changing our bodies and possibly our brains (Tangerman 2018).
- This screen time often leads to blurred vision, eye strain, and long-term vision problems like nearsightedness (Chen 2022).
- Screens emit blue light, which disrupts our circadian rhythms at night when we're trying to fall asleep (Putka 2021).
- A study supported by the NIH found preteens who clocked over seven hours a day on screens had differences in parts of their brains compared to kids who spent less time on screens (Naftulin 2019).

While VR may be a good tool for shorter periods of deep work—a few hours—clearly our current technology is not optimal for our brains and bodies. In the foreseeable future, most virtual work will continue to require us to look at screens—whether they be laptops, desktops, phones, tablets, or e-readers.

During the pandemic, many parents (myself included) witnessed firsthand what happens when we remove kids from an active physical school environment to stare at a screen for the entire school day.

One day in October 2020, I finished my first round of coffee and went through my email (yes—I like to get my shallow work done first thing), and went downstairs to check in with the kids. My eleven-year-old daughter logged into virtual sixth grade at an old dining room table on a tiny school-issued Chromebook. The screen showed a Hollywood-Squares-style Zoom call with the image of a teacher and black boxes with kids' names on them. My fourteen-year-old son sat across a partial room divider, on a repurposed desk, headphones on, looking at a similar tiny school computer with a bunch of black boxes.

My kids were disheveled, hunched over, yawning, and their eyes were glazed—but they were there, the wi-fi worked—and the class proceeded.

On a lunch break, I stood up to stretch my legs and went down to check on the kids. They were in exactly the same position as when I left them hours ago. They were not standing up. They were not moving. They weren't doing anything. It made me sad and frustrated to see them like this because I knew the teachers were doing their best, and my kids were doing their best, but it clearly did not work.

Over the course of the pandemic, my family struggled to keep active and moving. Coaches canceled sports, friends stayed in their houses, and kids no longer walked to school.

We were fortunate to have a home large enough for everyone to have their own space, and the sunny climate in North Carolina permitted frequent walks outside. Still, the kids struggled with their mood, and their learning suffered during the *lockdown*. I believe the brain-body disconnect contributed significantly.

When I considered ways people got creative and found new ways to thrive during the pandemic, I reached out to my colleague Danielle Vaeth. Prepandemic, Danielle was already working remotely for seven years and found a great rhythm to her work.

Danielle describes herself as a three on the enneagram–a system of personality typing that describes patterns in how people interpret the world and manage their emotions.

She is someone who focuses on efficiency and results. When I asked her about her prepandemic remote work style, she said:

"I've always been able to step away from my desk and go for a walk, go to a yoga class, just be out in the garden, or something to reset my brain and then just go right back to work."

When the pandemic hit, suddenly, all of Danielle's coworkers were also working at home, and her work changed. She noticed there were more and more meetings scheduled, largely as a way to keep people accountable who were normally in the office together. She noticed a sense of overwhelm, a growing type of GroupThink, and a Pavlovian response to the green light on her chat platform—a feeling of always having to be *on*.

"The more I hit the accept button on these meetings, the more I sat at my desk, the more inefficient I became, and I didn't even realize it. And so it almost became dispassionate for the work. My energy, drive, and joy at work all decreased without me even realizing it," she said.

Danielle felt like she needed to do something to get out of her pandemic routine. When she saw an opportunity to do yoga teacher training—a bucket list item—she took it. What happened next surprised her. Not only did the training help her mind and body, but it also improved her work.

"The yoga training unleashed me—I learned to connect to meditation and breath. I found this really assisted me with prioritizing my time, making me better under the stress of multiple commitments and my limited time. I had to fit yoga training into my day, and then I became more efficient at work. This helped me to choose how to spend my time and what projects I worked on. I started saying no to meetings or feeling I needed to participate in everything, telling others that 'it is better that I spend my time doing X, Y, and Z.'

"And as I started to say no to things, I increased the yeses that drew me into joy, energy, and drive. By making space, a shift happened. I reconnected and became much more efficient and effective at work. My creativity came back. I hadn't made space for it, being more focused on task completion than big-picture thinking," she said.

How did the yoga itself impact Danielle's experience of work—did her work improve because of increased movement? She emphatically said yes.

"I think the best way to describe what happened during the pandemic was a feeling overwhelmed by all the things I had to get done. This negative feeling transpired into a kind of tension within my body: my shoulders were sitting up a little bit closer to my ears, and my stance was more static in nature. These tensions are then related into sharp comments, a decrease in creativity, and a decrease in kindness. This changed when I started adjusting and moving regularly with yoga, both in the morning and in the afternoon or in the evening and started to create a practice. One of the greatest gifts I am still working diligently on is when I feel the need to speed up, which is frequent, I really need to slow down and get present. This becoming present brings me back to my body/brain connection," she said.

While Danielle feels the mindset shift of yoga and meditation was, in a way, the most important change, she also noticed the connection between her brain and her body. You may have seen the TEDx Talk by Amy Cuddy on Power Poses—how putting your body for two minutes in a power pose actually improves your performance (Cuddy 2022).

The connection between the brain and the body is powerful, and if we want to master the future of work, we must incorporate tactics that manage both the thinking brain and the moving body.

RECONNECTING OUR HUMAN BRAIN AND BODY AT VIRTUAL WORK

If you are curious to see how powerful the connection between the human brain and the body can be, check out the videos of the "Rubber Hand Illusion" (BBC 2010; Rohde 2011). The tantalizing rubber hand illusion (RHI) elicits the feeling a rubber hand belongs to one's body (feeling of ownership). RHI occurs when the experimenter strokes a visible rubber hand while synchronously stroking the participant's own occluded hand. In the videos, you can see the surprising effectiveness of connecting the rubber hand to the visual expectation of the participant's hand. Watch the fear when the experimenter hits the rubber hand with a hammer!

We can use our brains to get reconnected with our human bodies. We can increase the mindfulness of our own internal sensations. By practicing breathing techniques, like square breathing and alternating-nostril breathing, we can feel the connection between our breath and our arousal level. We can do body scans to check in with our internal state, and we can take movement breaks to stretch or move in a way that reconnects the mind and the body.

These practices are beautiful because they can all be done during the workday in quick one to five-minute breaks. Of course, we will have to step away from our desk/computer/devices to do them, so we will have to carve out time between meetings or work chunks (see section I of this book on time management).

Outside of the workday, we can also engage in activities to reconnect our brain and body. Almost any kind of motion can serve to reconnect. In my experience, the reason yoga works to reconnect mind and body is many of the positions are unnatural. The positions force you into challenging balances, where you have no choice but to pay attention to your body.

Even meditation and mindfulness exercises, without physical movement, can help reconnect our brain and body. Meditation helps to give greater insight into the (normal) human experience of constant thoughts coming and going. Mindfulness helps to focus attention on certain sensory perceptions which come in from the body, including things like taste and smell, which are typically subconscious.

I suspect with the current trends toward virtual work and virtual play, we will see increasing challenges with the mind-body disconnect. However, there will be more interesting research and tools available to help us reconnect the mind and the body.

Someday, we may find VR improves enough that our bodies feel like part of our virtual experience. This could bring together our expected bodily sensations with our other sensory experiences in a virtual setting, minimizing dissonance and easing the stress on our brain. We could replace verbal and digital body language with VR, letting the VR technology do the work for us. One downside of VR—it ignores internal sensations (at least in current iteration) like breathing and digesting. So it remains a fragmented version of the whole human experience.

CHAPTER 8

Cognitive Overload, Active Listening, and Silence

———

Merriam-Webster defines **communication** as *a process by which information is exchanged between individuals through a common system of symbols, signs, or behavior* (Merriam-Webster 2022).

The key term in this definition is *exchange*—giving and receiving information. Most people struggle to learn how to receive information. Without mastering listening skills, we are communicating *at* one another rather than *with* one another.

In Bellevue Hospital in New York City, on a fall day in 2003, I ran down the hallway trying to keep up with my patient Julie. She was rapidly pacing and gesturing wildly.

"Doctor, I am going to go get something to eat because the food is great. I like hamburger and did you know cows make methane gas? It is a real bummer that we are not taking care of the environment, and my college science class was so unfair because that teacher was mean—she had this terrible habit of pulling at her skirt and people were looking at her strangely, like maybe she was an alien and came from Mars, and there is a full moon tomorrow, and I love those werewolf movies..." she said.

"Julie, hold on a minute, I wanted..." I said. Before I could get another word out, Julie kept on talking.

"Oh yes, doctor, I really like it when we are talking because talking goes with walking and walking goes with running and races are fun and my boyfriend likes to watch boat races..." she said.

I tried to talk again. Julie kept on talking, and I ran behind her, struggling to keep up.

In psychiatry, we call this type of speech *pressured*. The listener feels pressed upon. They cannot get a word in edgewise. Pressured speech is a sign of mania. Patients with bipolar disorder who are in a manic episode will endlessly talk... and they utterly fail to communicate.

COMMUNICATION IS A GAME OF TENNIS, NOT GOLF

As a self-proclaimed nerd, I am not a big sports fan. However, I enjoy playing and watching tennis.

When I first started playing tennis in ninth grade at my public high school, my main goals were 1) to get out of my house after school, and 2) hang out on the tennis courts, which were yards away from the boys' soccer team practice. I never excelled as a tennis player—probably because most of my attention focused on the boys' soccer team—but I grew to enjoy the odd combination of solo and teamwork required on the tennis team.

At first glance, tennis is a solo sport. You practice tennis alone by hitting against a wall or with a ball machine. A funny thing happens as you get better at tennis. You slowly realize the way you hit the ball over the net is only part of the equation. You only have full control over the ball when you serve. When you actually play tennis, you start to realize you are interacting with another human being. You learn to watch them carefully and anticipate what they will do next. You learn their quirks and style of play. You manipulate them into making plays that are favorable for you and your style of play. Contrast this to golf, where ultimately, it is between you and the ball for how well you do on a given day.

When we communicate, we tend to think of sending out information. In my conversation with Julie, she sent out a nonstop stream of information, but there was no communication.

In the post-pandemic, virtual world, we think of all the different ways we can send out information—synchronously or asynchronously, written or verbal, visually or nonvisually. We forget communication includes listening and receiving information from the other person. We forget to build in systems to hear and understand each other. We forget to silence ourselves to better observe and process the information we are getting from each other.

As a result, many of us feel overwhelmed at work—too much information and noise and not enough true communication. We can understand this response through the concept of **cognitive overload**.

WE ARE VICTIMS OF COGNITIVE OVERLOAD

Cognitive load theory is a concept developed by Australian educational psychologist John Sweller in the 1980s (Lovell 2020). This theory proposes even the smartest minds have a limited capacity for new information within a given timeframe. It helps explain the cognitive demands on a person performing a complex task. Not surprisingly, the theory states that heavy cognitive loads or waves of complex topics without rest can push any individual to their own *cognitive limits*.

In this theory, there are three types of cognitive load:

1. **Intrinsic load**: An intrinsic cognitive load refers to the fundamental difficulty of a specific topic, regardless of the presentation of the topic. If you are learning calculus, the problem-solving resources needed to find a derivative will be the same whether your teacher clearly explains the topic or not. Your brain still must solve the problem using a combination of long-term memory, short-term memory, and strategic cognition. The cognitive ease of an intrinsic cognitive load will be the same regardless of external factors (although those external factors may add additional difficulties).

2. **Extraneous load:** An extraneous cognitive load refers to the *way* in which new information is presented, either by a teacher, a team leader, a colleague, a customer, or someone else. Visual learners easily process data presented as visual information. Yet, for auditory learners, visual displays may not be the most effective way to learn; for them, visual stimuli present a more demanding extraneous load.

3. **Germane load:** A germane cognitive load is the way an individual uses their memory capacity and personal intelligence to create mental schemas. Mental schemas are processes the brain uses to solve various problems presented by other types of load (we will discuss schemas in the next chapter). This type of cognitive load manifests when your brain develops a learning process to assimilate new information and use it to solve problems.

Cognitive overload occurs when the three types of cognitive load—intrinsic, extraneous, and germane—overwhelm a person. Cognitive psychology suggests even the most intelligent people can only process a limited amount of information at a given time. When bombarding an individual with competing cognitive signals, they struggle to filter relevant information from other stimuli. They may end up failing at a task or taking unnecessary actions on account of the cognitive loads clouding their judgment and abilities.

There are many examples of cognitive overload in the modern workplace. Common examples include:

- **Distractions:** *Social media and text messages can distract you from a task and make it nearly impossible to process information related to your job or education.*

- **Split-attention effect**: *Cognitive overload can occur when instructional designers create confusing learning materials. For instance, the split-attention effect results when one poorly integrates diagrams and written descriptions, forcing the reader to split their attention between the text and the image, which leads to cognitive overload.*
- **Expertise-reversal effect:** *In a classroom or work environment, the expertise-reversal effect describes how instructors can subject learners to cognitive overload by assuming prior information which the learners do not have.*

In the traditional office, cognitive overload happened; however, most people developed hacks. For example, to avoid distractions, they put the desk phone on busy signal, or they closed the door and moved objects off the desk.

To minimize the split-attention effect, they entered a conference room with others and only used a whiteboard to work together, putting away laptops and cellphones.

To avoid the expertise-reversal effect, a teacher read students' physical body language to look for signs of confusion, toning down the complexity of the material as needed.

During the pandemic, when people were working virtually, cognitive overload increased. In our homes, distractions were endless—phone, social media, pets, kids, lawnmowers, package delivery, laundry, etc. Most people had no way to manage these distractions; we tried to figure out virtual work hacks. On top of all the home distractions, the sheer volume of digital communication increased. Suddenly, workers felt bombarded with digital communication from multiple sources—emails, DM, text, and videoconferencing.

In addition to the sheer volume of incoming communication, the split-attention effect increased because the information came through a variety of digital tools, most of which were not synchronized or optimized for the individual's work. Managers forgot to check in for confusion and assumed that because they communicated digitally, the workers must have seen it, right?

I'm guessing you can remember many times in the past few years (or days) when you faced cognitive overload, a sense of overwhelm, and an accompanying sense of physical fatigue.

In 2009, Harvard Business Review published an article, *Death by Information Overload.* It showed the (circa 2009) surging volume of available information—and its interruption of people's work—adversely affected personal well-being, decision-making, innovation, and productivity (Hemp 2014). This problem became so important for organizations that Forbes published a 2020 article, *Why Cognitive Load Could Be the Most Important Employee Experience Metric in the Next Ten Years* (Freed 2020). This article cited cognitive overload as one of the biggest problems for organizations.

OUR BRAINS ARE OVERWHELMED AT WORK

On a good day, when we are well-rested, not distracted, emotionally grounded, healthy, and under low-stress conditions, our brains do amazing things. Before starting work on a task, our brains can choose which stimuli to pay attention to, set long-term goals which are consistent with our lives, prioritize which are important at the moment, and translate these priorities into work for the day. When we start to work on a task, our brains kick into gear. We select stimuli in our environment (words, images, and sounds), pay attention to the relevant stimuli, and place pieces of information into a mental workspace called working memory.

Much research exists on **working memory**—this term comes from psychology research in the 1960s. Interest in memory dates back to at least the 1800s. In experiments using simple stimuli, researchers estimated that working memory has a fixed capacity (of approximately three or four items' worth of information) no matter how long participants have to encode those items (Brady 2016). This means our brains can work on only three to four pieces of information at a time! Between the time you look at a seven-digit phone number and turn to enter the numbers on your phone, you may forget the phone number.

To increase the amount of information in working memory, our brains have different ways to *hack* the information by linking it to other familiar information already encoded in our brains. For example, we might remember the phone number 555-1776 as three fives and the date of the American Revolution, thus converting seven digits into two pieces of information. These hacks happen in the part of the brain known as the prefrontal cortex, as it connects at lightning speed with other parts of the brain, like the cingulate gyrus and the parietal cortices (Funahashi 2017; Chai 2018).

When we experience cognitive overload at work, our brain's working memory is completely overwhelmed. We try to cram ten to twenty multitasking elements into a working memory space designed for three to four items. A good brain hack can increase my working memory capacity to ten to fifty items. However, on a typical morning, I might handle one hundred emails while five DMs are arriving at the same time, while the dog barks, while the phone alerts a meeting in ten minutes. You get the picture. Even the best brain hacks cannot handle a constant, uninterrupted stream of communication coming in from multiple channels throughout a typical workday.

Regardless of whether we work virtually or in person, we must decrease the amount of information coming into our working memory. We must learn how to *close the loop* for each communication. When I receive a communication, I must have the space to listen, process, and then act or respond before moving on to the next task.

What it feels like to play tennis on a bad day: I feel overwhelmed by the ball rushing at me, I cannot process the movement, I swing wildly, and I often miss. I do not pay attention to the other person across the net from me, and I do not communicate. I am alone, overwhelmed, flailing, and doing my best to get the ball back across the net as quickly as possible with no particular aim or strategy.

Sound familiar? To enjoy tennis or work, I must manage the amount of incoming communication. I can turn my focus to the other person or people across the net or virtual workspace. What are they doing? Feeling? Thinking? Planning?

After I managed incoming communication, I learned to truly listen to other people at work.

PSYCHOTHERAPISTS TEACH US HOW TO *REALLY* LISTEN

As an overachieving ninth grader, I attended a calculus class in my underperforming public school. Being an unabashed nerd who loved math, I sat in the second row from the front, and I always raised my hand first to answer questions. Surrounding me was a room full of juniors and seniors who could care less about math and who were typically spacing out, doing their nails, or passing notes back and forth. In the front row were four well-meaning male students who wanted to do well in the class even though they struggled to understand the content.

Every day, I would eagerly raise my hand to answer a complicated calculus question, and… nothing would happen. The teacher was a middle-aged White man with classic nerd glasses and a pocket protector with pens on the front of his short-sleeved button-down shirt. He apparently did not think girls, especially ninth-grade girls, should be doing calculus, and he absolutely refused to call on me.

I experienced deep frustration and growing anger. It got so bad I stopped raising my hand and put my head down on my desk. Thinking I slept, my teacher would finally call on me, and I would pop my head up and give him the correct answer, then put my head back down. I found this highly satisfying, and my teacher found it highly irritating. He suggested to the principal I be removed from his class because I couldn't possibly understand the material he presented. Luckily for me, the principal suggested I take a standardized calculus test, which I blew out of the water. I stayed in the class, and the teacher would angrily call on me from time to time.

After this experience, I am not shy to make my voice heard. I learned how to speak up frequently in ways that were less offensive and more productive. *As I got better at speaking up, I got worse at listening.* I loved talking, sharing ideas, and connecting the dots. I would often forget to listen to the other person or people. My terrible habit of over-talking and under-listening persisted for the next decade into my twenties when I became a psychiatry resident.

During my psychiatry residency, active listening was one of the best tools I learned. As medical students, we trained in active listening to make patients feel seen and heard. Despite our training, most doctors stink at this, and bedside manner suffers in the era of seven-minute primary care visits. As psychiatry residents, the expectation was for us to learn multiple modalities of psychotherapy. We spent a lot of time listening to patients. Even though the different psychotherapy modalities (CBT, ACT, interpersonal, and psychodynamic) had different philosophical underpinnings, they all had one thing in common. The therapist must be a skilled listener. Therapists must take in information, process it, and effectively communicate it back to the patient.

ACTIVE LISTENING AT WORK

Carl Rogers and Richard Farson coined the term *active listening* in 1957 in a paper of the same title (reprinted in 1987 in the volume *Communicating in Business Today*). Practicing active listening also emphasized Rogers' (1980) concept of three facilitative conditions for effective counseling; empathy, genuineness, and unconditional positive regard (Leavitt 2002). Rogers and Farson said:

"Active listening is an important way to bring about changes in people. Despite the popular notion that listening is a passive approach, clinical and research evidence clearly shows that sensitive listening is a most effective agent for individual personality change and group development. Listening brings about changes in people's attitudes toward themselves and others. It also brings about changes in their basic values and personal philosophy. People who have been listened to in this new and special way become more emotionally mature, more open to their experiences, less defensive, more democratic, and less authoritarian" (Newman 1987).

In this framework, there are four components:

- **Comprehension**—this includes preparing to listen, paying attention
- **Retaining**—the meaning of the words
- **Responding**—tools include paraphrase, clarification, and summarizing
- **Assessment**—did the communication succeed?

In active listening, much of the content is nonverbal.

The listener observes the speaker's nonverbal behavior, body language, and tone (Maley 2012; Lackie 1977). Interpreting body language creates a more accurate understanding of the speaker's message. Body language conveys more meaning than spoken words (Atwater 1981).

According to a study conducted by Albert Mehrabian, 55 percent of communication is nonverbal. Nonverbal cues such as tone, inflection, gestures, and facial expressions provide the listener with further insight into what the speaker is trying to convey (UTPB 2020).

In the virtual workspace where we are working asynchronously, we are already missing 55 percent of normal nonverbal communication. In digital text-only communication, we do not hear the spoken word. As a result, we also miss inflection and tone. Miscommunication abounds in the digital, asynchronous space where words dominate.

Increasing the amount of nonverbal communication improves active listening skills in the virtual workspace. If your communication fails, you can shift *up* to include more communication information. For example, if you are on email and miscommunicating, switch to the phone. If you are on an audio-only phone and miscommunicating, switch to video. If you are on video and miscommunicating, switch to virtual reality. Finally, if you are on VR and miscommunicating, switch to in person. With each increasing step up, you will increase the amount and variety of communication you are receiving through your senses.

Another way to improve active listening skills in a digital, asynchronous space is to intentionally plan out the tactics for each communication modality. For example, if I communicate via audio phone, I map out my intentions:

- *Comprehension—this includes preparing to listen and paying attention*
    - I will turn off distractions by closing my computer and closing my eyes as I listen.
    - I will review the goals of the conversation in advance, so I feel primed to pay attention.
    - If I feel restless during the call, I will stand up and walk around my room so I can attend better.
- *Retaining—the meaning of the words*
    - I will have a piece of paper beside me and jot down any words which are important.
    - If there is a vague word, I will jot it down. When the other person is done talking, I will ask for clarification.
    - If I am a visual person, I will make a visual between important words with boxes, arrows, different colors, or other visual tools.
- *Responding—tools include paraphrasing, clarification, and summarizing*
    - When the other person finishes talking, I will say, "Here is what I heard…" and ask if this is correct.
    - I will ask for clarification of any of the words which were vague to me.
    - I will say, "So, to summarize, you think X, Y, and Z."
- *Assessment—did the communication succeed?*
    - I will confirm my understanding by stating a summary of what they said.
    - I will ask the other person if anything I said was unclear or if they have questions and pause to listen.
    - I will write down the takeaways or actions I need to take as a result of the conversation and put them in my daily organizer.

Creating a simple grid can help set intentions to actively listen in a variety of communication channels. I tried this first alone on different communication channels first to see what worked. As a next step, I introduced the idea to my team. Together we set intentions and practice.

Warning—this skill is difficult and requires practice!

CULTIVATE SILENCE TO COMPREHEND

In my virtual workplace, silence was difficult. Without body language, we miss social cues indicating when to speak and when to be silent.

When someone else spoke, I resisted the temptation to jump in and *add value* with my thoughts or beliefs. I stayed silent and used the time to get curious. I still felt uncomfortable, so I dug deeper. I asked myself:

- What is going on, and why am I having difficulty focusing on what the other person is saying?
- What are my body and mind doing while they are talking?
- What is my relationship with the person?

My findings surprised me. I had pent-up physical energy because I sat still too long. I was not addressing irritations with the other person. I felt insecure like I needed to add value to the conversation.

In researching this book, I learned that cultivating silence may actually improve equity in the workplace. Speaking all the time is a great way to suppress other voices. A classic example of silencing voices is the time it takes for a doctor to interrupt their patient. A 2018 study in the *Journal of General Internal Medicine* found that patients typically get eleven seconds to describe why they are coming in before the doctor interrupts them (Singh 2018). How can the patient's voice be heard in eleven seconds? What would happen if the doctor was silent for thirty seconds? Sixty seconds? Five minutes?

Whenever I talked, others couldn't speak. Whenever I blew up the group Slack channel, I buried other voices. I prevented others from speaking whenever I interjected my thoughts on the video call. Silence is an amazing tool for hearing voices we have traditionally ignored. Be silent, be attentive, and make it safe for other voices.

SUMMARY

As work is increasingly remote and asynchronous, opportunities to improve communication increase. We create a new normal at work by decreasing the amount of incoming communication and cognitive load. Less overwhelmed, we set intentions and practice active listening.

The more we practice active listening, we encounter moments of personal and interpersonal silence. We can thrive in remote work when we are silent and quietly absorb information. This silence is uncomfortable for many people, and they will typically rush to fill the void with other activities, like email, DMs, phone calls, and meetings.

Cultivating silence during asynchronous work periods is up to the individual. The individual must intentionally carve out time for silence and observe themselves. If you cannot tolerate silence, you are not alone. If you are like me, you must practice, starting with short periods of time and building to longer chunks of time. I turn off all notifications on my devices. I tell others I will be in a quiet place and am not to be disturbed. I use guided meditation apps. I go for a meditative walk in silence. I use my hands to do repetitive tasks while silent.

Cultivating silence during synchronous work like meetings requires leadership. Silence during meetings will encourage all voices, active listening between group members, and individual reflection on the topic at hand. If you are a leader, you experience firsthand how difficult silence is during meetings. As a leader, I identify a meeting facilitator. This can be me, a neutral person, or another person on the team with talent in this area. The facilitator guides the meeting and creates moments of silence. If we are using Zoom or other televideo, I say I will be muting everyone, and people should raise their hands to speak. When I need help, I ask for it. I find coaches or colleagues to help me brainstorm.

CHAPTER 9

Biases and Schemas

———

"Why do people expect us to learn new pronouns? They can't expect us to remember different pronouns for a given person on a given day. That is ridiculous!" I said.

We were sitting around the dinner table, and our food got cold. My teenage son shook his head. My teenage daughter said:

"Mom, what you don't understand is—gender and pronouns are a way for people to express themselves. It is about equity. You show people you respect them through the words you use."

The national conversation challenging traditional gendered pronouns perplexed me. I could not understand why young people found it so important to discuss their pronouns, change them, or request a neo-pronoun. I assumed the only people who cared about pronouns were transgender people. I thought they would be impacted negatively by people calling them the *wrong* pronoun.

What I learned through exploration and numerous conversations with my teenage children is—I fell into the trap of my own assumptions. I saw a dualistic gendered world where you prefer to identify as female or male. I understood a small group of people did not identify as one or the other, so they would be the only ones who cared about dualistic pronouns.

I now understand that young people see gender as an extension of equity and inclusion. By asking what pronouns an individual prefers, they are showing they are including the person in the conversation and they are respecting them as an individual. They are basically saying, "We are not making assumptions about you. Tell us more." They are trying to avoid stereotypes in their daily interaction.

While I still struggle with nongendered pronouns, my teenagers have forced me to challenge my own assumptions. I am more aware of my own internal bias towards binary thinking and what pronouns might mean to young people.

SCHEMAS ARE EVERYWHERE

A **schema** is a representation of a plan or theory in the form of an outline or model. When you make an assumption, you typically have a schema in mind, and you are trying to fit the data in front of you. *Humans have schemas for everything—* ideas (like my example of gender and pronouns), people, relationships, and much more.

One interesting example of schemas comes to us from the science of archaeoastronomy—how peoples and civilizations have looked to the heavens, designing architecture and tools to understand their world.

When you look up at the night sky, what do you see? You might notice how a clear, dark night reveals multitudes of stars, and you might imagine patterns in those stars in the same way you imagine images amongst the clouds during the day.

Constellations are one way in which people have imagined patterns and images in the night sky. These patterns literally and figuratively *connected the dots*—helping to make visual sense of the night sky and also to predict the world with science. If a constellation rose at a specific place in the night sky, it might be time to plant crops. If during another season, the constellation appears at a different place in the sky, it might be time to prepare for a rainy season.

Most ancient civilizations had constellations; however, the images differed from group to group. The constellations often reflected the religion of the society and connected ideas concerning religion to the natural world. For example, the constellation DRACO symbolized a serpent for the Greeks and Romans and a hippopotamus god for the Egyptians.

One fundamental concept in human cognition is our need and desire to project internal frameworks onto facts and observations. Schemas are mental structures we use to organize knowledge to help guide our cognitive processes and behavior. They can be both helpful and harmful.

When we use schemas, we can better understand the world around us through a way of understanding observations to guide our behavior. In the example of the constellations, people understood the movement of the earth through observing the position of the stars in the sky to guide their behavior to plant crops.

Malcolm Gladwell explained how we make decisions without rational thought in his book *Blink: The Power of Thinking Without Thinking* (Gladwell 2005). He compared the unconscious brain to a giant self-teaching computer. Malcolm said:

"The giant computer that is our unconscious silently crunches all the data it can from the experiences we've had, the people we've met, the lessons we've learned, the books we've read, the movies we've seen, and so on, and it forms an opinion."

While schemas can be tremendously helpful in crunching large amounts of data, they have a dark side. They can lead us to stereotype by making assumptions and using cognitive biases. Cognitive biases refer to how we pay more attention to information that fits our beliefs and ignore information that doesn't fit with our beliefs. We have all seen the harm they have created in our society—racism being an important example.

A human mind that has a hold over its prejudices is like the fabled philosopher's stone. Everything it touches turns to gold, whereas a savage mind run by its prejudices is like an infectious disease. Wherever it goes, it causes death and destruction.

—Abhijit Naskar, *The Shape of A Human: Our America Their America* (Naskar 2021)

Schemas are all over the place. For example:

- Google algorithms are designed to make assumptions about what we want to see—leading to increased political silos and decreased understanding of each other (Barrett 2022).
- Unchecked artificial intelligence is learning from human biases and worsening racial bias. For example, algorithms that review CVS discriminates against Black workers (Schulte 2019). Credit-scoring artificial intelligence (AI) discriminates against low-income individuals (Hao 2022).
- Physicians unknowingly treat Black patients differently than White patients when they are unaware of their own internal biases, and there are training programs to address this problem (AAFP 2020).

Maybe at this point, you are thinking, "But I am aware of my own schemas. I am not biased."

If so, I'm sorry to inform you that you are wrong. Even being self-aware does not make you immune from bias.

If you don't believe me, I encourage you to take fifteen minutes and take the free online Implicit Association Test (IAT) (Project Implicit 2022). The IAT measures attitudes and beliefs you are unwilling or unable to report. You will find it especially interesting if it shows you have an unconscious implicit attitude. For example, I believed women and men should be equally associated with science. However, my automatic associations showed I associated men more than women with science.

The IAT is surprisingly controversial (Sleek 2018). It makes people uncomfortable to think their brain spins stories subconsciously which are stubborn and resistant to change.

WHY DO SCHEMAS RESIST CHANGE AND WHAT CAN WE DO?

As I described above, our brains love schemas because they are an efficient way to process large amounts of incoming information. We take in sensory information—visual, sound, smell, taste, and body sensations—hundreds of times per second. The nerve cells in our bodies and brains fire rapidly to transmit this information through a combination of electrical and chemical signaling. All the incoming information must simultaneously be processed and connected with a variety of memories, goals, planning, activity, and communication.

As you might imagine, this takes a lot of energy. While the human brain only makes up 2 percent of our body weight, it uses 20 percent of our blood sugar (Mergenthaler 2013). If we did not have schemas in place as a mental shortcut, we would be overwhelmed by the incoming information and unable to take any action at all. Our ancestors in the jungle would be dead if they did not use schemas to connect the dots quickly between dangers in their environment and actions to avoid, escape, or conquer these dangers.

So, what can we do if we have a detrimental schema in place, causing us to make false and harmful assumptions? Cognitive behavioral therapy, or CBT for short, is one solution. CBT has become a popular type of psychotherapy because it is easy to understand and operationalize, and it gets results.

In CBT, the psychotherapist helps the individual take a deeper look at how their internal thoughts, feelings, and behaviors are linked. The patient gains insight. The therapist helps the individual identify changes they can make to their behaviors or thought patterns. In a final step, the patient does *experiments* in the real world. In each experiment, an old pattern activates, the patient becomes aware, makes a change, and then observes the outcome.

When I worked with patients, I enjoyed using a CBT approach. Sometimes the work proceeded slowly, and the patient's mindset was shockingly resistant to observation and change. At other times, an a-ha moment occurred, and the schema fell apart immediately. Through real-world experimentation, we can combat, shift, change, or even eliminate our assumptions.

CHALLENGING ASSUMPTIONS LEADS TO CREATIVE SOLUTIONS

Changing schemas and assumptions is hard work. When we challenge our own assumptions, we often unearth creative solutions which have a great impact at work.

During the pandemic, we all heard stories of how healthcare shifted to virtual, and suddenly everyone used telehealth.

Necessity suddenly upended the idea that healthcare must be in person, in an office, with a doctor doing a physical examination and all the trappings of a brick-and-mortar practice. Doctors, nurses, and other healthcare providers had to get creative and challenge their assumptions regarding what could or could not happen virtually. I faced a similar challenge to my own schemas of telehealth years ago.

In the fall of 2010, I entered my first year in private practice as a psychiatrist. Thrilled to operate my own solo practice, I could design the care I thought best for the patient. No boss, no hospital rules. Given that I completed a PhD in neurophysiology of selective attention, I found myself drawn to help people with adult attention deficit hyperactivity disorder (ADHD). Living in Chapel Hill, North Carolina, I located my practice down the road from the University of North Carolina. Put this all together—I treated many college students with ADHD.

In the month of April 2011, I saw these college students with ADHD for appointments combining psychotherapy, coaching, and management of their ADHD medications. The students arriving in April looked different. They were full of excitement with summer plans of internships, travel, and time to rest at their parents' home. They were also nervous and worried.

"Dr. Byrne, what am I going to do this summer?" one college student asked.

Confused, I said, "What do you mean?"

"Well, I am going home and then traveling. What am I going to do for appointments with you during the summer? I still need my medications, and I still need your help," they said.

Their question caught me off guard. Despite my careful planning, I didn't plan how to manage college students traveling out of the state. I knew the state medical boards and the psychiatric associations did not recommend treating patients over state lines except in the case of an emergency. I responded to the first student who asked me this question they should ask their primary care doctor to prescribe for them, and they should ask their old therapist to see them. I felt good following the recommendations and sent the student on their way.

Later in the afternoon, I got a frantic voicemail from the student. They said:

"Dr. Byrne—my primary care doctor at home already refused to help. My old therapist doesn't have time to see me. I tried to find a psychiatrist at home, but no one will see me for the summer. I don't want to find a new doctor for the summer. You know everything about me, and I trust you. Can't you call me or video me or something over the summer? Call me back, please!"

This gave me pause. What could I do next? Following the recommendations of the standard of care, I could say no to this student. They would run out of medication. They would be without help during a new experience. This made no sense because my patient needed my help. They needed to know I had their back. I researched articles discussing the (new) use of video calls to conduct psychotherapy and consultation appointments. I selected a modern building for my office and knew I had good internet connectivity. I knew the students also had good internet connectivity because they were attached to their phones and laptops all the time for school.

I called the student back and asked:

"Do you want to try a televideo appointment during the summer while you are out of town? If for any reason you need an in-person visit, you would need to go to a local doctor or urgent care center."

"Dr. Byrne, that is a great idea! So high tech—I call my parents for video calls all the time, so I know this will work," they said.

Over the course of the summer and the following summers, I experimented with the use of video to take care of my patients who were traveling for work or students who were off campus for breaks or internships. I figured out the details of scheduling, billing, which video platform to use, and how to document the need for video. I found the practice of video visits surprisingly straightforward. To my surprise, I enjoyed the video visits. I often learned more by seeing my patients in their own spaces rather than in my office.

Over the course of nine years, while I grew the practice, I saw an increasing demand for video visits. Patients, especially stable patients in a monitoring phase, loved the flexibility of video when they had a conflict at work, a childcare issue, or when they traveled. When it came time to renew my lease in

2018, I made a radical decision to shrink the physical footprint of my office. The future included video and did not require as many in-person visits. The landlord shook his head when I told him we didn't need the physical space.

Fast forward to the time of this writing in 2022. Most psychiatrists and psychotherapists are doing at least part of their practice via video. Many are not going to a physical office at all, preferring the convenience of working from home.

I shared this story as an example of when I was wrong, and my patients were right. My college students knew they would be better off if I did video visits with them while they were on break. In my old schema, all visits must be done in person. I had to see the patients in person and read their body language in order to diagnose and treat them accurately. I put my hand on their shoulder for support. I made direct eye contact to see if they were getting teary. I had a tissue box at hand and gave them a tissue when they cried. I showed up in my business clothes with my diplomas behind me. All these things were part of my schema—how successful psychiatrists worked with their patients.

My schema had social proof—generations of doctors before me trained on the superiority of in-person appointments. The state medical board codified these recommendations. Other psychiatrists in my professional society followed these recommendations. There were no articles in the literature with data examining the use of video to treat patients in psychiatric practice.

Despite the strength of my schema, both internal and external, it was wrong.

Carefully and anxiously, I challenged these assumptions with a few students in the summer of 2011. As time moved forward, I continued to challenge my assumptions of other use cases for televideo visits. I challenged my assumptions that video beats audio or phone only. I am still challenging my assumptions. Currently, I am experimenting with asynchronous communication (text and DM) and remote patient monitoring tools (apps) to efficiently and effectively work with patients.

HUMANS ARE IRRATIONAL

As a human being, I fall prey to my own schemas, biases, and assumptions. I always think of myself as a rational person. So, why am I so irrational? As someone who has researched how human brains work and practiced as a psychiatrist and a psychotherapist to change human behavior, I have seen firsthand how irrational humans can be. As a business leader, I use this understanding to improve my work with teams.

An entire branch of science emerged to understand better the irrational behavior of humans—at work, at home, and in the world economy. As the science of economy evolved, economists had wonderful models of the way markets should behave. In the real world, the models kept failing. Why? When they took a closer look, they understood humans did not behave rationally. Since the economy builds on a multitude of individual human decisions and behaviors, the economic model failed without accounting for the irrational behaviors of humans. The field of **behavioral economics** was born.

I sat down with Richard Mathera, one of the managing directors at Irrational Labs. We discussed how virtual work highlights irrational human behavior, and what we can do to fix it. He said:

"In the instantaneous transition from face-to-face first to remote first work, there has been a shift in the way we interact with each other in a work setting. I've seen a common behavioral principle that is pretty straightforward play out frequently.

"When something happens to me, largely I ascribe it to the environment. For example, let's say I show up late to a call. I know it's because I was busy on another call and juggling many other tasks. I'm overworked, tired, and trying to manage requests from everyone on the team.

"But when I show up to a call late, and someone else shows up to the call on time, they tend to ascribe my tardiness to me rather than to the environment. They might think, 'Richard isn't responsible. He doesn't show up on time.'

"In general, when things happen to us, we tend to ascribe them to external forces. But when things happen to other people, we tend to think that that's a representation of them as a person rather than the external forces that have acted upon them."

Humans frequently make this psychological bias—named the **fundamental attribution error**. Curious, I asked Richard if this error changes when people are working remotely. He said:

"Yes, I think technology exacerbates this. When you're face-to-face in an office setting, you have these moments where you start to learn much more about the world of the person that you're interacting with. Maybe that person has two kids, and you know that their kids are going through challenges. You start to think that this is going to impact their ability to show up, or maybe they're going to get distracted and have to go take care of something at home.

"In an in-person environment, the salience of a person's situation outside of work increases, informal rapport naturally increases, and I think this somewhat mitigates the fundamental attribution error, and we're more likely to give someone the benefit of the doubt. But with technology, there's much less ability for us to interact informally and naturally get cues about the other person's environment. And then I think the consequence is that the fundamental attribution error likely gets exacerbated."

I agree with Richard's observation that virtual work changed the way we learn about other people. We ignore signals concerning their personal life, forget to ask questions, or make assumptions. However, there is a positive flip side to this error.

Research showed women, people of color, and other minorities post-pandemic have found working remotely advantageous. At remote work, the fundamental attribution error applies in a more equitable manner.

For example, many women leaders were frustrated by their male colleagues inadvertently passing them over for promotions and opportunities. This came from a kind instinct. The men assumed women needed to spend more time with their kids, so they didn't give women more work. The men assumed women probably didn't want separation from their families, so they didn't ask the women to travel. In other words, men made assumptions that the environment dictated women's behavior, especially when married or a mother. For men, behavior reflected character. For women, behavior reflected the environment. I experienced this personally as a woman in a professional setting.

In early September 2006, I completed my psychiatry training in New York City, and my husband and I made a leap of faith and moved our little family to North Carolina. My son had just turned two, so many big life events were happening all at the same time. We had one week to purchase a home, we needed to buy a car, and we needed to find a nanny or daycare. Things got more complicated en route when my maternal grandmother died unexpectedly during our family beach vacation, and I became pregnant with our daughter.

We showed up at a new job in a new city in a new house with no friends or family, no furniture, no car, a two-year-old, and a new baby on the way. The decision of how and when to tell my new employer about my pregnancy troubled me. I wanted to make a good impression and to make sure they didn't limit my patient caseload because I would not make enough money to pay the bills. I also worried about how and when to tell my new patients about my pregnancy. Would they trust me to treat them after I had the baby? I had worked so hard for so many years in my career, and I didn't want problems.

Happily, I found my voice and was quite assertive regarding my pregnancy and what I wanted to get out of the job. Luckily, as the only psychiatrist on the team of doctors, they badly needed my help managing all the mental health issues their patients faced. I built my caseload without difficulty over the next few months.

Then things got even trickier. By December, I was visibly pregnant, and I endured an endless stream of commentary at work. "Are you sure you want to see these patients? Are you able to walk and make rounds? When are you going on maternity leave? Can I touch your stomach?"

My daughter, like my son, arrived early, and I gave birth the week before Christmas. As a healthy preemie, she needed to feed and grow, so she stayed in the hospital for a few weeks.

At work, people made all sorts of well-wishing assumptions about what I wanted. They assumed I wanted to sit beside my tiny daughter at the hospital all day long. They assumed I wouldn't be able to see patients in their homes because I would be breastfeeding all day long. They assumed I wanted to take three months of maternity leave. They assumed I didn't want to work. None of these assumptions were true.

Two years earlier, after the birth of my son, I followed the assumptions of other people. I was miserable. This time I knew what I wanted. I wanted my husband to have time with our daughter since his job in NYC did not permit him to have time after the birth of our son. I felt physically great and I wanted to work. I needed the income from work. I hated being at the hospital all day because it implied something was wrong with my daughter.

I hated the assumptions concerning me as a new mother. I wished my employers and colleagues had asked me curious and nonjudgmental questions. What did I need and desire? I wished they focused on my patients' outcomes, not my motherhood.

Imagine a future of work where we do not make assumptions about our teams, colleagues, and bosses. What would it look like?

INTENTIONAL SYSTEMS TO OVERCOME ASSUMPTIONS

When I considered equity in the workplace, I immediately thought of Natasha VanWright. Natasha has many degrees to her credit—RN (registered nurse), MBA (business administration), MS (health care administration), and an MA (nursing education). In her current role as vice president of care management, her pragmatic empathy stands out.

I asked Natasha how she overcame assumptions in a systematic way at work. She described how she trained her teams of care managers. Instead of making assumptions about how they will learn the best, she asked questions, designed, and iterated.

"Different people learn differently. They learn at different paces. They process information in different ways. It takes people so much longer to understand a concept if you approach them from a learning style that doesn't suit them." Natasha said.

Natasha described different types of learning styles—using written words, visual cues, or physical tools. She pointed out that one individual may have one dominant learning style, or they may use different learning styles for different content. In developing her training, she had several steps. She said:

"The first training I did was about personal learning style. We talked a little bit about the different types of learning. We said very clearly that one person might need to learn information one way, and another might need to learn it in a different way. And in doing that, the objective was one, to make people aware, like 'Oh shoot, I really do have a pre-ferred learning style,' and two, to also let them know that it is all okay. We let them know that we're aware of your learning styles, and we're going to adjust this training based on your learning style."

So, Natasha avoided making assumptions about learning styles. She systematically determined individual learning styles and normalized them for everyone on the team. What she did next was even more remarkable.

"We created the training with different components: some PowerPoints, some role-playing exercises, some visuals, some actual documents, and some step aids. It approached learn-ing in different ways. As a next step, we did check-ins as the training proceeded to ask, 'Is the content moving too fast or too slow? Do you like the way it's delivered? Do you think it could be delivered in a different approach?'" she said.

In other words, Natasha did not assume the training drove the desired effect—she planned to check in and iterate as needed. She took the time and effort to avoid making assumptions up front. She avoided assumptions as the training proceeded. Natasha noted two surprising outcomes. She said:

"Since we were doing training virtually, I thought that there would have been more variance in how people responded. I thought I would need to make a whole lot of changes to the material, and we didn't. And I also thought that people would need more breaks, like for those kinesthetic learners who need to move around. But people really wanted to plow through many things.

"Many of our team came from face-to-face settings. They assumed that our virtual orientation was going to drone on and on. So, getting people out of their shells was a problem in the beginning. People expected us to throw content at them and ask questions and try to get them engaged and involved in the learning. Coming from a virtual environment, I also wrongly assumed that people would be okay being virtual and wouldn't have any problems expressing themselves or saying, hey, I have a question or pause there. But in the beginning, it was hard for some people."

I love Natasha's approach to a new, virtual modality of training her team. She never made assumptions. She continued to take the time to check in, asked people how things were going, gathered data, and made observations. Using this tactic, she successfully iterated her work product while at the same time making everyone on her team feel seen, heard, and appreciated.

SUMMARY

We know humans are hardwired to use schemas, make assumptions, and be generally irrational. Sometimes these schemas help us, like conserving time and energy, and sometimes they hurt us when we make incorrect assumptions and errors.

However, there is reason for hope. Humans are also capable of insight and can be remarkably flexible to change engrained thoughts and behaviors, like with cognitive behavioral therapy. There are pragmatic ways to challenge schemas and assumptions at work, and while they take time and energy, the payoff is big. Creativity is one example.

As my colleague Natasha aptly said:

"I think these were things we should have been doing all along. When we look at children, they know how to play and learn things in an out-of-the-box manner. But as they get older, we train them to make that box smaller and smaller. All the creativity and, you know, all the unique things that different people bring to the equation never happens because we've negated it."

In the next chapter, we will dive deeper into our assumptions concerning working in homes versus working in offices.

CHAPTER 10

Overcoming Assumptions about Virtual Work

———

When my teenagers highlighted my lack of understanding of pronouns, I felt embarrassed. My stomach clenched, my face flushed, and my shoulders hunched up. Luckily, the stakes were low for our pronoun conversation. Being wrong felt much worse when I fumbled business decisions based on my incorrect assumptions. I wasted tons of time and money.

In the spring of 2019, I had a tough decision. My outpatient psychiatry practice of nine years grew from exactly zero patients to over 800 active patients. My team grew from exactly one person (me) to eight employees. I self-decorated an absolutely beautiful office space on the top floor of an environmentally friendly, high-end building. My expensive lease came up for renewal, and all signs pointed to growth. A few years early, I doubled my office space. I saw the increased footprint as a marker of success, and I felt proud.

Looking at the numbers, it made sense to grow my office's square footage. But something felt wrong. There were many days when I came into the office and half the offices were empty. Business was good. What happened?

The future of work infiltrated my beautiful workspace. My employees opted to work from home for a half day or a whole day a week. Patients increasingly asked for televideo appointments rather than coming into the office in person. All our operations, including our phones and electronic health records, had moved to the internet cloud. We saw more people doing their consent forms via e-signature. We scanned and uploaded medical records without a paper copy in sight. Our shredder sat empty. We got rid of our industrial-sized printer/copier and bought small cheap printers.

I approached my landlord on a sunny March day and sat in his large, equally beautiful office space down the hall. I told him I wanted to downsize my office space.

Shocked, he said, "Why on earth would you want to do that? Is the business not doing well?"

We walked together down the hall to my practice. White noise machines hummed quietly, and I pointed to all the empty rooms.

I said, "Do you see what is happening here? All the doctors are at home seeing their patients via telehealth. Most days, we are at 100 percent capacity for patient appointments, but only at 50 percent capacity of people using their offices."

My landlord looked at me like I was nuts. "Why don't the doctors want to come to their offices? It is so peaceful and beautiful here," he said.

I smiled and said, "Because sometimes home can be peaceful and beautiful. When the camera turns off, you can take breaks and go outside. You can pet your dog. You can run a quick errand if your patient cancels their appointment. My doctors value this flexibility just as much as their patients."

When I looked back, the signs were clear. We made assumptions concerning the future of work that were simply not true. We made decisions based on an old, antiquated model of nine-to-five factory workspaces. We didn't see how getting out of a physical office space, even a beautiful one, helped many people in many situations.

WHY WE GOT IT WRONG

In my house, we call the prepandemic world the *before-time* and the post-pandemic world the *after-time*. We have trouble remembering the way we thought back in the before-time. People in the before-time operated under the assumption work needed to be physically bound in an office space. However, a small number of people worked at home.

Larry English challenged the status quo. In his book *Office Optional*, Larry described the successful virtual company he built over the past twenty years, stating, "We accidentally found the future of work" (English 2021). Ironically, he published this guide to virtual work in early 2020, before the pandemic forced the majority of the world population to work at home.

Larry's experience mimicked my own observations within my office in 2019. He pointed to the signs of a shift to remote work in the prepandemic world:

- Sixty-nine percent of Gen Z and millennial managers let their team members work remotely.
- Twenty-three percent of workers reported doing a portion of their work remotely.
- By 2028, 73 percent of all departments will have remote workers.

Larry wanted to build a company that reflected his values and felt thrilling every day. He said:

"All of us experienced an incredible amount of stress in our previous roles, and while stating a new business can certainly create its own kind of stress, we didn't want to bring those old pain points into our new company. And we certainly didn't want our future employees to experience the same.

"We just wanted to create a great environment. A couple of years in, we looked around and realized how happy we were. Over time, we've realized that having a great culture does more than make work enjoyable. It's actually a big competitive advantage."

Larry's words resonated with me because I started my business in 2010 with the goal of creating a great place to work. Traditional health care settings felt wrong to me. I picked a beautiful office space because I wanted to come to work, feel calm and collected, and surround myself with beautiful things. As I started hiring employees, I wanted them to feel the same way. I wanted them to feel supported to practice medicine the way they wanted. I wanted patients to walk in the office and feel respected in a consistent, professional manner.

At the time, I assumed the physical office drove the culture I built. I was wrong. We can create high-culture, mission-driven, aesthetically pleasing workspaces without going into a formal office space.

Where did the assumption we needed to work nine-to-five in a physical office come from, anyway?

In the nineteenth century, the Industrial Revolution engulfed Europe. People worked hard, eighteen hours per day, six days a week. One of the founders of socialism and an influential British politician, Robert Owen, believed people should follow a different schedule:

- eight hours of work
- eight hours of leisure
- eight hours of sleep

Robert Owen presented this model to the British government as early as 1817. It failed. He eventually convinced the government to reduce the workday to ten hours per day for women and children in 1847. Fast forward to 1905. Henry Ford made the most significant change to help his workers—he reduced the workday to eight hours—and still turned good profits.

In 1938, the American government passed the Fair Labor Standards Act of 1938. The American government changed the maximum working hours to forty-four hours per week and created overtime pay, whereby anything after forty hours was paid double.

Over the past century, many jobs in the United States shifted away from factory work and toward other forms of work that involve a variety of administrative tasks. The factory nine-to-five model stuck with us, even as jobs moved off the factory floor, up and out into office buildings. The traditional office became engrained, ultimately spoofed in pop culture hits like the 1999 movie *Office Space* (Judge 1999), the 2001 BBC (Gervais and Merchant 2001), and the 2005 American series, *The Office* (Daniels 2005).

These pop culture creations signaled the end of the traditional office. We enmeshed ourselves in this office culture, and we didn't realize a different way existed. We watched pop culture and laughed at the ridiculous office culture. However, we still couldn't imagine a future of work without the traditional office. We just laughed and stayed stuck in our own assumptions.

Pop culture was able to do what academics and business school gurus could not. They showed the traditional office as an outdated concept, filled with silly and harmful assumptions about the meaning of work.

VIRTUAL WORK LEVELS THE PLAYING FIELD

When we dig deeper, we find good reasons to dispose of the traditional office. As with many traditions, traditional office culture served to reinforce traditional power dynamics and inequities.

Physical office spaces typically include conference rooms, where teams can assemble to meet in person. A well-known psychological phenomenon of the conference room is the *power seat effect* (Tirado 2012). Whoever had the most power in the room sat at the head of the table, sending a powerful social cue. Others viewed them as the leader, in control, and ready to intimidate. People saw those who sat in the middle of the conference table as approachable, friendly team members who were there to collaborate. Similarly, in many office spaces, the size and the location of an individual's office indicate their power and influence within the organization.

In the past, office designers tried all sorts of creative design solutions to get around these social cues and the psychological impact they had on workers. Feeling left out because you sat in the middle of the conference table? We made the table round. Feeling like you are missing important conversations because your office was on a different floor from the CEO? We made everyone sit in an open floor plan.

Of course, these tactics failed. Big circles or U-shapes replaced the rectangular conference table, and people screamed at each other across the table (Rattner 2019). Open floor plans, initially hailed as the workplace of the future, ended up creating negative psychological effects, making workers feel less productive and more distracted. Workers got sick more frequently and felt pressured to work longer (James 2021).

We were all missing the point. The traditional office did not succeed for many people. It failed human beings who all have their own needs, preferences, and work styles which are optimally productive for them as individuals. Even worse than low productivity, the traditional office created environments that were inequitable and discriminatory.

As part of the process of writing this book, I had the pleasure of working with Jacqueline Calamia, a developmental editor. In addition to being a supportive and curious editor, Jacqueline has a warm and relatable energy that comes through loud and clear. Jacqueline is also disabled, uses a wheelchair, and is not able to drive her car due to epilepsy and cerebral palsy.

Jacqueline enjoys the flexibility of working from home in her current job as an editor. Even prepandemic, Jacqueline worked from home on her own schedule. Prepandemic, she only found two companies willing to let her work from home. She chose this position because they did not see her disability as a barrier. In fact, they thought her experience as a disabled person could be an asset in working with other authors who wanted that perspective.

I asked Jacqueline about her experience as a disabled person watching the able-bodied world forced to suddenly work from home. She said:

"[Able-bodied] people are starting to realize some of what it's like to be a disabled person. I heard people talk about how weird it is to be at home all the time and not to do things we're used to doing. The disabled population found this *normal* because many of us get out a lot less often than our able-bodied coworkers or friends."

With regards to working from home, Jacqueline found it interesting and frustrating. The disabled community told people that for years remote work was possible. Nobody believed them. After working remotely during the pandemic, many friends came to her with the realization that remote work is possible and it's not as hard as they thought.

Jacqueline was optimistic for the future because she noticed the rise of remote work leveled the playing field for disabled people. She said:

"People are less focused on whether or not you can get to the location in order to do the job or how long it takes you to get the job done. They are more focused on whether you have the skills to do the job. It's all about 'Can you get the work done to this to the level we expect from you.'"

Remote work offers the opportunity for a level playing field, especially as it relates to appearances. When focused on the skills and the expectations, suddenly it doesn't matter what you look like, how you speak, or how polished you are.

Speaking with Jacqueline, I reflected on my past experiences of appearance at work. As a woman, when I worked at the hospital or an office, I had to focus on my appearance in a way that my male colleagues did not. In the hospital, I made my hair presentable and put on makeup, even if I dressed in wrinkled scrubs after sleeping in a call room overnight. In the office, as a young woman who was both a business owner and a leader, I needed proper dress and appearance.

During the pandemic, dress codes confused me. I didn't know what to wear—weird. I had casual clothes for weekends and formal clothes for work. I didn't feel pulled together for work wearing my weekend clothes, and I felt too formal at home in my work clothes. This silly problem revealed the hidden costs of being a professional woman. I could see where not polishing your daily appearance saves a lot of time and money. Working remotely also makes it easier for people who feel judged about how they look. I believe this is particularly impactful for women, people of color, and others who are more likely to be judged on appearance at a traditional office.

I am happy to report that I have figured out what to wear. Now, I largely dress to please myself. Some days I might put more time and effort into appearance. Other days may be low time and effort on appearance. Jacqueline had a deeper insight—for disabled people getting up and dressed and out of the house can require tremendous effort and preplanning. Working remotely, she noted people could decide how much effort to put into their appearance.

She summarized it beautifully and said:

"I think that people are getting a lot more comfortable just kind of being themselves."

In the future, if others judge our work more on skills and expectations and less on our appearance, we move to greater equity in the workplace. Working outside of the traditional office already had tangible benefits for many people.

Despite the mental exhaustion which video calls can create (see chapter 5), when used thoughtfully, video calls can reduce traditional power structures at work. Well-run video calls include a facilitator who navigates power plays, making sure everyone has a voice. The boss looks like everyone else on video. There is no power seat or corner office to display. Groups feel *flat* with less of a visual reinforcement of the vertical power structure within many organizations.

Adding private, asynchronous time for workers creates a virtual office for everyone. Importantly, there are no cubicles in the virtual office. We assume all workers show up eager to talk, eager to interact socially, and eager to work together in groups. In reality, some people have a more introverted work style. They need time to step back and process information. For these individuals, virtual work can be a blessing. They have asynchronous time to slow down, be alone, and process information.

Companies like Insights help teams understand individual work styles and learning styles (Insights 2022). I remember completing this assessment and being surprised. Within the Insights system, many people are *blue* and prefer to take away information and spend time alone to process and produce work. We assume people's personalities are *red* (quick, decisive, bright) or *yellow* (social, wanting to work with others) because these people typically talk the most and get the most attention in the traditional office.

The careful design and iteration of asynchronous work tools like Slack or Miro allow teams to engage all team members, allowing for personal preferences and optimal work styles (Slack 2022; Miro 2022). Of course, the devil is in the details. Virtual teams must be extremely thoughtful in how they use virtual work tools. Facilitators are often needed to ensure smooth execution.

Honestly, shouldn't we have been carefully designing our workplace all along?

BRINGING YOUR WHOLE SELF TO WORK

I loved my beautiful office space. I have fond memories of the design, the furniture I hand-picked, and the way the reception felt. If I am honest, my beautiful space created problems.

When I started my practice in my thirties, I looked younger. As a young female professional, I accepted the premise that appearances really mattered. I arranged my beautiful office so I had the big CEO office at the end of the hall, and I made sure I sat at a desk so patients would see all my framed diplomas behind me. I dressed formally, with great care to being put together and attractive without giving the impression of being too attractive or too fashionable. I squeezed myself into Spanx. I wore heels. Full confession—I actually fell down a flight of stairs in my three-inch heels during a fire alarm evacuation of the beautiful office.

I spent a lot of time and energy planning my presentation and appearance in the workspace. My daughter encouraged me to wear fun nail polish, and I said:

"I'm sorry honey, I can't wear neon green nail polish at work."

My story ended well. As a young female physician and entrepreneur, appearances did matter. I carried myself well and was successful. Patients and other professionals took me seriously and respected my work.

How would this story have played out in a virtual office? Appearances still mattered, yes, but off camera, I dressed more comfortably, and no more falling downstairs in heels. I wore brightly colored nail polish. I decorated my home office the way which feels right to me, and no one has seen my diplomas. I brought my whole self to work, and it has largely been positive.

Reflecting on myself ten years ago, it makes me a little sad. What if I didn't spend so much time, energy, and money on appearances? What if people looked at the quality of my work first and my appearance second? What if I had more fun and expressed my personality more during the weekdays? Could I have had more success and more fun?

As part of writing this book, I spoke with many colleagues, many of them strong women leaders. Perhaps not surprisingly, these women shared stories about how they let down their formal facade and brought more of their whole selves to the virtual workspace.

Dr. Grace Terrell is a force of nature. I admire her forthright and authentic approach to leadership as a woman physician who has taken on multiple roles, including CEO of a large, multistate healthcare organization. When I asked Dr. Grace about her experience with gender roles and leadership in healthcare, Dr. Grace told me a story. She said:

"My daughter is an attorney, and her husband is a data analyst for a company, and they both took twelve weeks of maternity and paternity leave when my granddaughter was born. When they returned to work, we were in the middle of the COVID-19 pandemic, and there was no childcare available for various reasons until the baby was six months old.

"So, I went to Boston for one month to help them out. I took my computer, and basically, I did not stop the work I was doing. In between work, I was changing diapers and thawing out my daughter's breast milk and feeding it to my new granddaughter. And, you know, it was a wonderful experience for me. I was able to help out my family, and I was able to have that time with my granddaughter.

"At the time, I was working with a group of great people in India, and I told them I would continue to work and most of it would be asynchronous. But when we're having meetings, there may well be a baby there and she may well be crying or spitting up. So, during meetings, there were many times when my granddaughter just sat on my knee. She looked at the camera and the people on the screen. And what was interesting was that my Indian colleagues loved her. Sometimes she fussed, and we had to reschedule our meeting, but that was okay."

Knowing Dr. Grace, the image of her at a business meeting with a baby on her knee, made me smile. I asked what her Indian colleagues thought of seeing her in a different light.

"One of my colleagues made an interesting observation. He said that when the baby was there and I would go into Grace-CEO-mode and out of Grace-Grandma-mode, the baby would cry every time.

"She knows," he said. "Your voice is different, and your body language is different."

"It was kind of interesting. He observed this happening, and I did not. It was an interesting time of having to blend some of the different aspects of who I am. I had to stop wearing my normal dark professional shirts and wear white because the baby kept spitting up on them!" she said.

As a highly successful woman leader for decades, I wondered how Dr. Grace experienced bringing her full self to work and showing the different sides of her to her clients.

"Would you consider showing up in a different way to work in the future?" I asked.

"I always try to choose who I show up as and where I show up. It may not be obvious, but I'm more introverted than most people think. So, I'm pretty careful at making sure you know I am authentic and real in any situation I'm dealing with, but there are parts of me that I would not necessarily show or share because it might not be the right environment for it. In that situation with my meetings with clients in India, I was in two modes simultaneously, and I thought I was doing pretty well with it. But the baby certainly noticed the disconnect. So perhaps I will learn from that," she said.

Dr. Grace's interactions with her Indian clients gave them an opportunity to empathize. They did not make assumptions about how Dr. Grace would handle meetings and work. Dr. Grace did a fabulous job of setting expectations in advance. They were curious and observant. They noticed how the baby reacted to Dr. Grace when she exhibited different modes. She was the beneficiary of their empathy and kindness, and it enabled her to have a highly meaningful three months of her life taking care of her granddaughter.

I asked, "So, how did your Indian clients like working with you in this way?"

I could hear Dr. Grace smile over the phone.

"Oh, they absolutely loved it. I feel like I am much closer to them as a result of them seeing me work in this new way," she said.

I imagine many people, men and women, experienced bringing their whole selves to work during the pandemic. Like Dr. Grace, many of us assumed we had to bring a highly curated and polished version of ourselves to the office, then take off the costume and be a different version of ourselves. We are better off without this false assumption. People who were not traditionally in powerful positions, like women and minorities, prefer virtual work because they are less *on display* than at the traditional office. They report fewer micro-aggressions and fewer biases (Tulshyan 2021).

Some people value privacy and will choose to continue to have a separate *work self* because it psychologically makes sense for them. Others, like me, are bringing a more fully synthesized version of themselves to the workspace. I no longer have a beautiful office space. However, I love my home office because it feels like a full version of me. I no longer squeeze into Spanx and heels unless the mood strikes me. I can even paint my nails neon green with my daughter.

SUMMARY

In the prepandemic world, most people, myself included, assumed the traditional office with a nine-to-five schedule was desirable, if not absolutely necessary. Signs surrounded us—this work model failed many people, and some companies had embraced virtual work with strong outcomes. Outside of pop culture, most people ignored these signs and continued to work in a model based on factory work centuries ago. Few questioned this model because they enmeshed themselves so deeply that they couldn't imagine anything different.

The pandemic forced us to challenge our assumptions about virtual work. For most people, leaving the traditional office felt uneasy and even disturbing. People with social work styles found the lack of constant social interaction difficult. People with more reflective and introverted work styles enjoyed the individual and asynchronous work options.

One of the side benefits of virtual work is an opportunity for a more synthesized version of yourself at work. This may favor people who are not traditionally in power positions in the workspace, like women and minorities. Virtual work also opens doors for people with disabilities and levels the playing field—perhaps accelerating a path toward a more equitable workplace.

CHAPTER 11

Identifying the Limitations of Empathy

———

ROBOTS FAIL AT EMPATHY—BUT HUMANS CAN BE TRAINED

One myth about psychiatrists and psychotherapists is they are naturally empathetic 100 percent of the time. That has never been the case for me.

In the summer of 2002, I returned to my clinical rotations after I completed a grueling five-year PhD in neurophysiology. Simultaneously excited and terrified, I worked at a shabby and friendly family medicine clinic on the Lower East Side of Manhattan with a kind young male family doctor.

On my first day at the clinic, I vibrated with nervous energy. After spending the past five years with other researchers and my rats, I was frustrated with my human interaction skills. I felt my teachers did not prepare me to sit with patients. I did not have a template to write notes. I couldn't find the exam equipment. I was angry and unempathetic with the patients and the staff working in the clinic.

By lunchtime, I worried I had made a terrible career mistake, and I would not complete medical school. My kind supervisor asked me to sit with him at lunch and chat. He asked about my experience in research and said:

"I can only imagine what it must be like for you here today after being in the lab for so long."

He gently reminded me that most medical students felt this way on their first clinical rotation, and he struggled at the beginning.

He spent the next hour asking what I needed help with and patiently reminding me how to write a visit note. He demonstrated true empathy and kindness at the moment I needed it the most. By the end of the day, I felt better and less terrified. By the end of the first week, I completed simple tasks with ease, and I started rebuilding my own empathy skills with patients.

Empathy is a skill I mastered over the years. However, I continue to practice on a regular basis. To this day, I still fall into a judging rather than learning mindset. I trained and grew my natural empathy. If it is not continually observed and practiced, it will atrophy and judgment will replace it.

Empathy training is now a scientific discipline. There are a variety of research labs doing work on empathy; for example, the **Stanford Social Neuroscience Laboratory** looks at the nature and consequences of empathy (SSNL 2022). They say:

"Audience members' palms sweat while they watch a tight-rope walker teeter over a precipice. Friends wonder how to help each other through struggles, and customers wonder whether a used car salesman is genuinely happy to see them. All these instances represent forms of empathy: sharing, thinking about, and feeling concern for others' emotions.

"We study empathy through a wide range of approaches and methods. We differentiate between different *pieces* of empathy, such as vicariously taking on others' feelings (**emotional empathy**), thinking about their experiences (**cognitive empathy**), and feeling the motivation to improve their well-being (**empathic concern**). Our work probes the brain processes that support pieces of empathy and use computational models to describe how people make sense of others' emotions based on facial expressions, language, and other cues. We're also interested in when and how empathy leads people to accurate versus inaccurate impressions of what others are going through, with an eye toward improving interpersonal understanding.

"Our lab also explores the benefits of empathy, for example, in reducing individuals' stress and building relationships. We are also interested in the noisy but powerful role of empathy in guiding moral decisions."

Based on the work of the Stanford lab and other groups, we are beginning to understand the neuroscience of empathy. If we understand empathy to be a normal part of human experience, we can design and measure interventions that train and improve empathy between individuals and within communities.

You can likely think of times in your life when others have shown you empathy. It is baked into many *good manners*—to open doors for people carrying big boxes is a simple form of empathy. It feels wonderful to receive empathy.

There are many ways to train empathy without studying as a psychotherapist. The Stanford lab also designs **empathy training** using virtual reality (VR), which has real-world applications. One interesting training uses VR to help individuals experience homelessness. After the VR training, a significantly higher number of people signed a petition supporting affordable housing for the homeless (Herrera 2018).

Whereas the Stanford study used VR to train *normal* people to empathize with the homeless, other VR formats can be used to train people with Autism Spectrum Disorder to improve their real-world empathy skills. Teachers use Class VR with autistic children to improve empathy for both students and their teachers (Paiva 2022).

Outside of clinical and research applications, there are many types of non-VR empathy training available. The training focus on communication, emotions, or community. Often empathy training is part of programs designed to improve your EQ or *emotional intelligence*. Empathy training has become a buzzword in management training during the last few years. Many managers struggled with questions of "what do I do?" or "what do I say?" in response to world events like COVID-19 or racial injustice.

Empathy in the workplace is not new. It was there all along—we weren't paying attention.

Others often ignored leaders and managers with *high EQ* in favor of more operational and financial skills. Despite evidence from Harvard Business school demonstrating leaders with low EQ and high skills had a failure rate of 25 percent, most companies don't train EQ (Fernández-Aráoz 2014). We did not see the value of *soft* skills of EQ in building and retaining top-talent teams at work.

Robots suck at empathy—and research argues empathy acts as a principle limit for AI (Montemayor 2021). Neuroscience shows empathy likely relates to the same neuronal structures and networks which we use to mirror behavior in others (for an example of how mirror cells relate to Zoom fatigue, see chapter 6). Christian Keysers of the Netherlands Institute for Neuroscience in Amsterdam wrote a nice summary (Armstrong 2017) of this phenomenon. He said:

"We also activate our own actions as if we'd be acting in similar ways. We activate our own emotions and sensations as if we felt the same."

Through his work at the **Social Brain Lab**, Keysers, together with Valeria Gazzola, has found observing another person's action, pain, or affect can trigger parts of the same neural networks responsible for executing those actions and experiencing those feelings firsthand.

For example, if you watch a video of a person using their hand to grasp toy balls hidden in a bin, your brain will mirror this activity in your motor cortex. You use this information to gauge the other person's confidence in their ability to pull out the ball. In another example, people without empathy (antisocial personality disorder patients) lacked normal brain activation in their anterior cingulate cortex when they viewed an aggressor twisting another person's hand.

As Bill Clinton famously said, "I feel your pain" (C-Span 1992). When you see another person in pain, your brain will respond empathetically, and you will also feel pain at a neuronal level.

The design of our brain mirrors behaviors we see in other humans. This skill gives us an evolutionary edge because we can quickly learn new behaviors which are adaptive to our environment. Humans are not alone in the ability to empathize. Elephants, dolphins, whales, chimpanzees, and a handful of other animals also demonstrate emotional reactions resembling empathy and self-awareness. They recognize themselves in the mirror, they mourn the death of their young, and they experience a wide range of emotions.

An article in HuffPost made the argument nonhuman animals may have a greater capacity for empathy (Hunnes 2017). Another study found that humans have atrophied their empathy ability, resulting in a variety of societal and environmental problems (Rutkin 2013).

In the past few years, we saw a resurgence of interest in empathy training among leaders and managers. Despite this good news, most training failed to highlight an important fact. Empathy is a limited resource.

EMPATHY FATIGUE IS REAL

In my private practice, I offered psychotherapy to my patients. Having done my psychiatry training in New York City, I did a ton of psychotherapy training. I spent many years learning cognitive behavioral therapy, psychodynamic psychotherapy, and other types of supportive psychotherapy.

I first started my practice with a small caseload. I had maybe fifty patients in total, and most of them liked to do psychotherapy with me. A typical psychotherapy session would be forty-five minutes with the patient and then a ten-minute buffer between appointments. At first, I saw four or five people a day, and I loved it. The connections with my patients energized me. I had no burnout, and I had high empathy.

Over the next few years, my practice grew. I saw more patients per day. Typically, I had a caseload of 150 active patients, and a third needed psychotherapy at any given time. My days got longer and packed back-to-back with appointments. As many of my initial patients stabilized, we switched to shorter *medication management* appointments. During these shorter appointments, I spent twenty minutes with the patient, with a ten-minute buffer. I could only handle one to two longer psychotherapy appointments per day.

So, what happened? Why could I only see two patients for psychotherapy without feeling tired at the end of the day?

What happened was **empathy fatigue.** As a psychiatrist and a psychotherapist, I trained in empathy fatigue. Psychotherapists are human beings who can take on only so much in a single day. To be honest, in psychotherapy, the emotions were strong. I felt fatigued when I took on other people's emotions, put myself in their shoes, and saw what they experienced.

When I looked closer at my practice experience, my empathy level decreased when I saw patients for medication management. Even though these patients were not being seen for psychotherapy appointments, they walked into the room with stories and emotions and things happening in their life. Despite the shorter appointment length and focus on medications, I still found myself empathizing with them. I took on emotional content, even though I didn't practice psychotherapy, per se.

A typical medication management appointment lasted thirty minutes in total. I had, let's say, four hours of those a day. Eight people deserved my empathy. By the time I got to the psychotherapy patients, I couldn't handle more than two in a day. I saw how empathy fatigue arose from medication management, which in theory, should have been cut and dry.

Understanding empathy fatigue helps us understand our struggles in the workplace. I read many articles discussing the need for empathy from managers and leaders. People are currently on video calls for hours and hours, trying to exude empathy through the camera.

Even great leaders only have so much empathy to give in a single day. To maximize the amount of empathy we give in a day, we have to take really good care of ourselves. We must be physically, mentally, relaxed, rested, calm, and collected. We have to show up in an incredibly good state of mind.

Managers and leaders in the workplace can learn from psychotherapists how to manage empathy fatigue. Cleveland Clinic psychologist Susan Albers recommends an ABC model for coping with empathy fatigue (Cleveland Clinic 2021):

- **Awareness.** Acknowledging how one is feeling and showing oneself compassion is key. Often the best thing we can do is to take a moment to actually feel our emotions and sit with them.
- **Balance.** Do you have other interests besides your job and taking care of other people? Is there a balance between worrying about others and your self-care routine? Returning to the basics and focusing on what we can control can be helpful.
- **Connection.** In a world where social distancing is the norm, it can be challenging to feel connected—but doing so can be a solution for those experiencing empathy fatigue. Albers recommends reaching out and having conversations with people you care about or considering connecting with a professional.

When I work with healthcare organizations that employ psychotherapists, leaders are puzzled why psychotherapists normally work thirty to thirty-five hours per week. I explain psychotherapists are not lazy, nor do they hate the forty-hour work week. Psychotherapists succeed when they manage their own empathy fatigue. Psychotherapists need five to ten hours of work time on a weekly basis to process their own emotions, do self-care, and connect with others.

One common practice of psychotherapists which can be beneficial to managers and leaders is **peer supervision**. In peer supervision, a group of psychotherapists meets for one to four weeks for a few hours. They discuss difficult cases and new treatments. Mostly they share the emotions and the experience of being a psychotherapist. They intentionally connect to share compassion. Finding time to regularly and intentionally meet with peers outside of your organization to discuss your experience as a manager or leader can be powerful. I found peer supervision in the workplace: in small coaching groups, social events, or other types of networking.

Psychoanalysts are one type of psychotherapist who focuses on a type of psychotherapy called psychoanalysis or psycho-dynamic psychotherapy. Psychoanalysts are concentrated in New York City and have a wonderful practice of taking the entire month of August out of the office. This **mini-sabbat-ical** helps them rest and recharge their batteries so they can sit with challenging patients who come to see them two–five times per week. The concept of the mini-sabbatical (a break less than six months long from work) gained traction in other settings as a way to counter burnout (Singhal 2021).

Finally, psychotherapists train in **countertransference**—the idea that our own internal conscious and unconscious schemas and biases directly impact our emotional response and empathy. If we lack awareness of our own countertransference, it harms our relationships. If we are aware of our own countertransference, it is a powerful tool. For example, I learned when I worked with a patient with borderline personality disorder, I would suddenly forget all the details of their case. Despite not knowing how this schema arose, I learned to recognize it in myself. It became a helpful tool—forgetting details.

Training and nurturing empathy are not as simple as it seems. I saw examples of empathy executed in a clumsy way. Sometimes, I didn't check myself, and I ran out of empathy with others at work.

EMPATHY IS NOT A CHECK-THE-BOX, ONE-SIZED FITS ALL EXERCISE

Being a leader during the pandemic created many challenges. These challenges persist as many teams are working virtually. When I sought a bird's-eye-view of current leadership challenges, I contacted Jane, an executive coach who worked with C-suite leaders.

I asked Jane, "What do you see with the leaders you coach?"

She said: "My feeling is that people are trying to figure out what that means to be a better human in the workspace."

"The pandemic put an extra-strength magnifying glass to work cultures, highlighting how well-equipped organizations were to handle human needs. At first, an almost instant camaraderie developed around the shared experience of barking dogs and kid voices. Within time though, the burden of the bottom lines and business deadlines revealed that many companies' claims of recognizing human needs was really just lip service.

"Now, over two years later, we're seeing talent voting with their feet and choosing companies where being human is not seen as an acceptable condition, but rather an asset. And the leaders who are emerging as most successful are those who can see their employees simultaneously as experts in their field and humans and are able to address their needs on both dimensions."

Jane shared a great summary of the state of **humanism** at work. Humanism is an outlook or system of thought attaching prime importance to humans rather than divine or supernatural matters. Leaders tried to focus on humanism at work. However, we did not train our managers and leaders on how to execute this new skill. Jane found many of her clients tried to learn humanism in the virtual setting. They struggled. Sharing a recent story concerning one of her coaching clients, Jane said:

"I shadowed a C-suite leaders team meeting. My client was leading the meeting and trying to connect; peppered throughout the meeting were clearly elements that this woman felt checked the box on humanity.

"In this meeting, let's open it up. How's everybody doing? Here's a picture of my job. Oh, this is Jenny's dog. You know, look how cute, does anybody else want their dog profiled in the meeting? Silence—then moving on to—here's a topic you know, specifically substantive concept. Here's introducing a new team member. That person then has to say five things about themselves, and you know nobody really felt like they knew this woman much better as a result of that.

"Later in the meeting, there was a *two truths and a lie* thing. Later, they got to whole survey data from a culture amp survey that they had done. When this happened, I thought to myself, *Okay, this is going to be the moment where there's discussion.* There were slides and metrics.

"Then my client asked 'What questions do you all have?' And it was total silence. My client then moved into OKRs, showing what was green, yellow, etc. The meeting ended with my client saying, 'Wow, this is miraculous that I'm giving you six minutes back.'"

I experienced similar scenarios frequently in my own meetings. I saw meeting leaders run through a checklist of activities—ultimately failing to demonstrate humanism. I was curious if Jane thought her client would have had the same difficulty in the old-fashioned in-person setting. Jane thought this woman had obviously been successful in her career in a *buttoned-up* kind of way. Other people expected her client to be more humanistic, more personal, and more vulnerable. Jane focused on coaching her client through this difficult transition.

Leadership at work has different styles. In the past, leaders focused on results, keeping their personal life private. Perhaps with a shifting generational demographic at work, a new focus on mental health, and the Great Resignation, people talked about "bringing your whole self to work." Studies showed it required less effort (especially for women) if they showed up to work as a whole self and didn't feel like two people, one at home and one at work. Jane pointed out the flip side to this whole self-at-work movement. She said:

"I also think the pendulum has swung in terms of bring your whole person to work concept and what that really means. People feel on the one hand they do want to be seen for things that go on for them outside of work, but they don't want to necessarily have to be required to share those sorts of things. From a leader's perspective, how do you walk that line of *I'm supposed to be interested in who you are in your whole self,* and *if I don't acknowledge that I'm going to run afoul of empathy or vulnerability connection?* But, on the other hand if I do ask I might be probing where someone else might not be interested in my probing; and at the end of the day, we're here to get a job done. Right?

"I think this aspect really is messy because I think everyone is trying to do the *right* thing. Of course, there is no one right way, and it is hard to understand what each individual needs and how much they want to share. Finally, you can spend so much time on that effort on being humanistic, that it leaves less time for the actual work that is supposed to be the reason everybody is assembling in the first place. So, I think that's really hard," she said.

When I consider Jane's stories, my heart races and I feel anxiety in my body.

We can train our managers and leaders to grow and sustain empathy, and it does not require of school. There are four main steps:

- Understand what empathy is and why it is important.
- Believe we can train our empathy, even if it has become atrophied.
- Learn what steps are needed to cope with empathy fatigue.
- Check ourselves—be self-aware of our own *stuff* getting in the way of empathy with others.

Years ago, I managed one male physician (not a psychiatrist) who learned how to manage teams of health care providers in a complicated matrix organization. Despite being an amazing clinician and a brilliant thinker, he appeared to have low EQ and atrophied empathy. When we first met, I saw him painfully blunder in his efforts to get a new clinical program off the ground. He bulldozed over coworkers in his way. After months of carefully planned operational detail and financial planning, nothing happened. Why? Because his operational plans were not empathetic. He did not take the time to actively listen to the clinical teams, and he did not put himself in their shoes.

Happily, this physician leader wanted to improve his skills, and he made tough changes to his own leadership style. I spent several months exercising my own empathy as his manager. I actively listened even when I wanted to jump in and give him advice. I checked myself when I slipped into a judgmental mode or made assumptions. I took my time, and I took care of myself. I made sure to show up calm, cool, and collected to our meetings. I spent the time to ask other people in the organization how he interacted with them. I specifically focused on getting to know him as a person, and I used StrengthsFinder as a tool to see where his strengths lay as compared to others on her team.

I spent three months working hard on the EQ side of the relationship, and then he shifted. The investment of time and effort led to a profound sense of trust. This man showed vulnerability with me, we trained his empathy muscle, and he saw results. His clinical program picked up steam, and he developed relationships with peers who became his advocates in the organization. Since our time together, he was promoted and now manages his own team. I hope he continued to build his empathy muscle because if he combined EQ skills with his other leadership skills, he would be a powerful force in healthcare.

SUMMARY

At work, aiming for empathy all day long leads to empathy fatigue. We need more empathy training sessions to discuss empathy and fatigue, and to plan for a realistic amount of daily empathy:

- How much empathy are you really able to give?
- What are you going to do to take care of yourself to maximize empathy and recharge the battery?

Managers and leaders struggle with learning empathy fatigue, and it may require working less. To maintain high empathy at work, we might spend more time taking care of ourselves, or resting, or relaxing, or doing other things. This may sound counterintuitive. Perhaps we have seen managers who try to force empathy too much when a lighter touch would have been better.

When we have fewer conversations, we can make them higher quality and more empathetic. Then, we can spend less time on check-in emails. This in turns saves time at work, so we can replenish our empathy reserves outside of work.

In short, when we train our empathy, we should make sure we're also training for empathy fatigue and how we will avoid it.

CHAPTER 12

Empathy Tools

Empathy is a buzzword these days. One would think it would be a must-have skill in the workplace. Unfortunately, it's not.

In fact, empathy levels are falling. A meta-analysis of US citizen empathy test scores found the average American today is less empathic than 75 percent of Americans thirty years ago (Konrath 2011).

But there is good news. You don't have to be a trained psychologist to learn to use empathy at work.

EMPATHY COMES IN THREE FLAVORS

If you are looking for ways to build empathy in your workplace, you should first understand the three types of empathy (Bariso 2018):

1. **Cognitive empathy** is the ability to understand how a person feels and what they might be thinking. Cognitive empathy makes us better communicators because it

helps us relay information in a way that best reaches the other person.

2. **Emotional empathy** (also known as affective empathy) is the ability to share the feelings of another person. People have described it as "your pain in my heart." This type of empathy helps you build emotional connections with others.

3. **Compassionate empathy** (also known as empathic concern) goes beyond simply understanding others and sharing their feelings: it actually moves us to take action, to help however we can.

Typically, when people discuss empathy, they describe cognitive or emotional empathy. Emotional empathy appears more often as a trait, but it can be trained. Psychotherapists are a great example of people who train to have emotional empathy (as I described, I was not naturally emotionally empathetic before my training). The popular idea of empathy often focuses on cognitive empathy: if we can get a better mental understanding of the other person or people, then we are being more empathetic.

Looking at art can help train and develop empathy. If you take the time and effort to engage with a piece of art, you are putting time and effort into engaging with the artist, with their subject, and with the history of the piece itself. These are all empathy skills.

Winter holidays in Chapel Hill, North Carolina are typically not filled with magic snowfall. On December 22, 2021, we came out of a rainy weekend and started a balmy 55-degree sunny morning. Itching to get out of the house, I took the family to the Nasher Museum (Nasher Museum 2022), a small art museum at Duke University.

This museum displays older pieces; however, it also focuses on presenting newer artwork, much of it with a social message. On this day, the art did not put me in a calm zone. I felt slightly unpleasant. It wasn't until much later I realized the source of the discomfort.

When I look at neoclassical painting like Jacques Louis David's 1787 *The Death of Socrates*, I am interested in the history and symbolism of the painting, in addition to appreciating the artist's technical ability (David 1787). In other words, I connect with the piece primarily on a *cognitive* level.

When I look at art filled with luminous color like Rothko's 1958 *No. 16 Red, Brown, and Black*, I am pulled into the painting with an emotional experience. I project my own *emotions* onto this nonfigurative space (Rothko 1958).

At the Nasher, I looked at pieces like the 2015 piece *Ain't Gonna Let Nobody Turn Us Around* by Hank Willis Thomas (Willis 2015). This piece uses mirrors to pull you into the narrative of the Civil Rights March in 1965. While I didn't have a strong emotional response or a strong cognitive response, I did feel something. I felt an urge to act. *This contemporary art is political and made me feel I should take an action.*

We are all struggling with empathy in the virtual workplace because we are missing out on compassionate empathy.

How can we create more compassionate empathy at work? A manager can train on how to ask better questions, be better listener, and to convey emotional connection with their employees; however, this will only take you so far. We miss the actions which show we care and understand.

FINDING EMPATHY IN THE NEW OFFICE

In the traditional office, small acts of kindness and empathy were more obvious. You held open the door for people carrying boxes. You brought someone a cupcake on their birthday. You gave someone a pat on the shoulder when they look like they need support. You handed someone a tissue when they teared up.

In the workplace of the future, we need to rethink compassion. We can offer small acts of compassion in the virtual workplace. We offer to open a virtual door by taking small task off their plate. We send a happy birthday note in the mail to a teammate. We can use emojis wisely to convey support or other emotions.

A bigger and more interesting challenge is how organizations can show compassion to their employees. We continue to struggle with organizational empathy. The actions of an organization make a statement concerning empathy toward its employees.

For example, people right now search for increased flexibility and autonomy at work. When considering organizational action, we need to rethink basic assumptions around time off and incentives:

- Why do we need PTO?
- Why don't we say, "I expect you *not* to work X number of days per year."
- Why do we assume single people don't need leave time the way parents do?
- Why do we assume financial incentives are more meaningful than nonfinancial incentives?

Like the nine-to-five workweek, the history of **Human Resources (HR)** (Human Resources Degrees 2022) reveals the origins of these assumptions. In the early twentieth century, HR ideas came into fruition with the rise of trade unions and personnel management departments. Early HR related back to the idea that treating workers as people lead to better business outcomes. It reacted against the Industrial Revolution when work conditions were extraordinarily poor, and workers were treated as disposable commodities.

By the middle of the twentieth century, universities taught HR and HR departments became a part of corporate America. These days, most large companies have a separate HR department with *business partners* tasked with managing all the people issues in the organization. People argue HR departments are no longer needed and HR should no longer be a separate group (Marr 2018). Rather, they should embed it within each functional unit of the organization.

I agree with this formulation—the *people* function of HR is not a stand-alone siloed task. Everything an organization does depends on people—unless your organization is run by robots. This idea that empathy is present in all work correlated to the way the human brain processes empathy.

Looking at the brain, we see multiple brain areas involved in empathy. There is no HR part of the brain.

1. **Cognitive empathy**—the human **neocortex** (specifically the frontal lobe of our brain) is involved in the thinking part of emotion. What in my past experience gives me clues of what the other person is thinking?
2. **Emotional empathy**—the **amygdala** is an older part of the human brain and is directly connected to emotions. What am I sensing from the other person who is triggering an emotional response inside of me?
3. **Compassionate empathy**—the **motor cortex** and **cerebellum** are action centers in the human brain. They take instructions from other areas of the brain or reflexes to plan and execute actions. What actions do I need to take to show the other person that I see them and care?

Being empathetic requires all three parts of your brain. The successful expression of empathy involves a coordinated brain effort. Humans do not possess a separate little piece of our brain which we turn on and off when we want to be empathetic! Encoded throughout the human brain, this is visible in the *mirror cells,* which help us mirror other humans. Mirroring cells exist in a variety of locations in the human brain.

We continue to learn the neuroscience of empathy; a 2018 article showed researchers used imaging studies to better understand these brain functions (Mackes 2018). This article found cognitive empathy to be as important as emotional empathy when trying to understand other people's emotions.

In other words, multiple parts of the brain worked together create empathy for others.

IS EMPATHY THE NEW WATERCOOLER?

Many of my consulting clients say one of their biggest concerns regarding distributed work is the lack of the office watercooler conversations. They remember the in-person setting where you would run into someone unexpected in the hallway and have a quick conversation which seeds a new idea. They remember times when a coworker would come by your office and say, "Hey I am running out to get lunch, want to come with me?" They remember the simple tactic of putting free food in the breakroom and watching people congregate.

Without these informal moments, many managers and leaders worry about their team cohesion. They worry ideas stagnated. They worry that we missed the human part of work. They worry that their teams functioned like robots without human social connection.

As a psychiatrist and a psychotherapist, I see how difficult empathy is for people in the virtual setting. If you can't read a coworker's body language, or bump into them in the hall for small talk, or see a photo of their family on their desk, how do you get to know them? How can you be empathetic without understanding who they are?

I currently work with an organization tackling this question head-on. This company is distributed, so they do not have an actual watercooler. In addition to adapting good IM practices for casual conversation (see section on communication), they have tried different ways to get to know new team members in the virtual setting.

The company leaders found they could create empathy using an online collaboration tool. They searched for ways to whiteboard virtually, missing their whiteboard from a physical office. As they learned to whiteboard with Miro, they got curious and excited. They investigated learning modules on how to collaborate virtually.

Their first attempts at virtual whiteboarding were basic—a whiteboard where they drew and created boxes with arrows running back and forth. After a few versions, they became more sophisticated. One leader found a template which encouraged the use of an icebreaker, and he tried it out in a small group.

I must confess, I am not a big fan of icebreakers. When in person, I find icebreakers silly and awkward, trying to get people comfortable with each other and rarely succeeding. However, in the virtual setting, the icebreaker did something completely different.

On a first icebreaker we shared our favorite food. Silly, it made us laugh and learn a little about each other. On the next icebreaker we shared one of our favorite childhood movies and why we liked it. We used a visual tool to put a photo or image representing the movie on the virtual whiteboard. I picked *Girls Just Wanna Have Fun*, a terrible and wonderful 1980s movie I loved as a tween girl. When I put the image of this movie on the board, it brought back memories for me. I smiled and shared these memories with my colleagues. Then I listened.

I learned one colleague grew up on a farm. I learned another colleague loved outer space. I could hear in their voices (we were doing a synchronous meeting sharing screen with voice only, no video) how the childhood memories made them feel. Not having to look at each other while sharing this memory made it more powerful. When I closed my eyes or looked at the movie image they put on the whiteboard, I imagined their experiences. If I had to look at them in the face or make eye contact, I would not have been transported. In the same room, I would have been paying attention to their body language and it would have distracted me from their story.

This phenomena really surprised me. I got more out of a ten-minute icebreaker on a virtual whiteboard than I had after months of knowing my colleagues. I felt more of their emotion, and I imagined them as a child. This is what empathy does. It makes you understand the feelings and experience of another human being. Because of the emotional and experiential content of sharing, you understand the person better. It makes it easier to work together, because you make fewer errors of assumption, and you can more readily put yourselves into their shoes.

I am optimistic for empathy in the virtual workspace. Finding virtual tools to connect, to understand each other, and to share emotion are the keys to building empathy.

Bell Labs used an unusual office space, leading to increased collisions and dramatic creative advances. At this company, the laboratory spaces were connected to a single, vast corridor, longer than two football fields. This accident of architecture led to an unexpected side effect. To get anywhere—scientists literally had to walk by the open doors of their colleagues in different functional areas. They spent time with more people, and they learned about different parts of the organization. The frequent unexpected collisions led to more empathy, more empathy led to more trust. More trust led to creative (and profitable) outcomes.

Another example of how to build empathy comes from medical residency training. In a three-to-four-year residency, young physicians rotate through a variety of medical settings. We learned different fields and different types of patients. When I completed my psychiatry residency, for example, I spent long chunks of time with different teams in neurology, internal medicine, emergency medicine, and intensive care. By spending time with different teams, I developed a great sense of empathy for these other physicians, their teams, and their patients. To this day I can quickly put myself in the shoes of other physicians who are not psychiatrists.

ACTIONS SPEAK LOUDER THAN WORDS

Perhaps you have made progress at being more empathetic with your emotional nuance, you have improved your active listening, and your communication skills are better, and you want to take it to the next step—action.

For many people, actions build trust. Actions build the feeling of you *have my back*, you are thinking of me, you are seeing and hearing me, you are taking steps to demonstrate compassion.

In the summer of 2020, America faced a racially charged situation, and many people took to the streets to protest racism in America in the George Floyd protests (Taylor 2020). Most organizations wanted to do the right thing, and the organization where I worked wanted to show support for the anti-racist movements throughout the country.

Reacting quickly, the leadership of the organization planned a company-wide webinar event to discuss this topic. I felt proud of how decisive and bold the leaders were. They were willing to tackle the hard issues even if they made mistakes. As the question of what to do and what to say arose, many leaders thought the best choice would be to ask Black employees in more senior positions to come and speak at the webinar.

The leaders attempted to be empathetic with words, to say we were supportive to all employees. In reality, these words ran false. Instead of considering, researching, and asking what our Black leaders and employees were experiencing in the moment, we made an assumption. We assumed they would want to speak up and share with the entire organization.

If we created a better space for active listening, we would have understood many of our Black colleagues were experiencing the events as a trauma. For some, the last thing they wanted to do in that moment was stand up and make others else feel better when they themselves were hurt and struggling.

Happily, we had strong Black leaders in our organization who were able to articulate this without being prompted. Some did want to speak, and others did not. In hindsight, we weren't demonstrating empathy through our actions. It would have been more empathetic to understand the important issues to our Black employees and leaders, and with our actions given them the time, space, and support they needed. I/we missed the mark. I am grateful for the grace my Black colleagues showed in that moment.

So, who is getting it right? What organizations are hitting the mark on actions which demonstrate empathy and compassion to their employees?

As part of writing this book, I met a fellow author, Arin Fordstadt. Arin is a millennial who recently entered the workforce during the COVID-19 pandemic; all her work to date is in the virtual setting. She is also an energetic, talkative young woman who shows clear passion for helping people with mental illness. Since Arin's college education and internships were in a different field, she returned to classes which will prepare her for a graduate degree in psychotherapy. Arin loves her new virtual job which has nothing to do with her passion.

"I decided I was going to get a remote job that worked with my time, not my passion. I wake up every single morning and I have not once wanted to dodge logging into work. The company I am working for is the gold standard for what people think of when they think about a healthy and diverse corporate culture," she said.

Arin described how the company made her feel valued and supported. They took a proactive stance toward time management and personal growth. When it came to valuing Arin's time, the company was highly flexible since day one. She said:

"I was very clear when I interviewed that I was starting grad school. I also love to travel. So, I may just move across the world, and I may be gone for a month." I told them, "If this doesn't work for you, let me know."

They responded, "Sure, that works!"

Arin was pleased the company had stuck to its promise, even when she traveled to Europe for a month in the summer. Her boss didn't respond with anger, trepidation, or concern. They told her to text them the week before travel to notify them when she would be out of the country. Excited, Arin considered other opportunities.

"Then I decided, if I push grad school off, I can still travel. I can move across the world and travel because my job allows for that. I told my boss, 'Hey, I'm thinking of moving to Europe from September to December.'

"And they said, 'Okay, cool. Let me know if your hours may need to be adjusted to fit your time schedule better.'" she said.

For Arin, this flexibility and the company's positive attitude toward her desire to travel or live abroad signaled that they valued her as an employee. They valued her desire to travel. Their actions showed her they were truly empathetic.

Arin also shared a great example of how the company demonstrated empathy around time management. She said:

"The biggest thing is that the expectation is not for you to work outside of your hours. The company knows that in the virtual setting, it is hard to sign off work when other people are still working and that people worry they will be seen as lazy if they sign off right at the end of their scheduled work hours."

Laughing, she told me a story. She signed on to the virtual work platform three minutes after her work hours schedule ended. Her friends from work immediately sent her a message "It's 5:03 p.m. what are you doing still logged on to work?" She felt positive peer pressure to sign off work and leave for the day.

Arin's examples of why she loved her company relate back to empathy and shared trust. They showed her empathy through flexible work hours, supporting her passions, and setting expectations not to work all the time. These actions may sound simple. However, they were highly impactful for Arin and others at her company:

"For me, this job is the perfect job because I'm not burnt out. I'm making solid money: enough to pay back my loans, enough to pay for grad school, and enough to live my life and move across the world. I work with great people, really truly great people who are there to help me. They're allowing me to grow and explore and experiment within my own journey."

I believe there are other organizations—like Arin's—who are actively making changes, so work does not suck for their employees. In the next section of this book, I discuss what the future of work might look like when managers and leaders are proactively shaping their teams to manage their time, communicate effectively, and show empathy at all levels—cognitive, emotional, and compassionate.

SUMMARY

Over the past few years, and perhaps as a direct consequence of the pandemic, people have a better understanding of empathy.

Empathy training has progressed. Managers and leaders acknowledge empathy is no longer a *soft* skill. Empathy has escaped the silo if HR departments. While learning how to actively listen and to communicate clearly and with respect matters (part II), individual and organizational actions also matter.

We need to go deep into organizational assumptions and challenge them to redesign work with empathy in mind. Join me as we take a look at what the future of work can look like for our organizations and us.

CHAPTER 13

The Future Is Now

The old ways of working were outdated. Trailblazers recognized this before the pandemic.

People are considering ways to work virtually or in a hybrid manner where a group of people are physically together, and others are virtual. Even though geographically distributed teams have been working together for centuries, we weren't paying attention. The pandemic put the spotlight on distributed work.

Distributed groups of people use different time chunking strategies to get the most out of their in-person time and their individual deep work time. By chunking deep work and social work time, our brain improves attentional focus. We can be more productive with less time at work. When we are designing our virtual or hybrid workspaces, we should look for answers from brain and behavior science and organizational psychology rather than business-as-usual best practices.

PIONEERS IN HYBRID WORK

In 2000, things were going my way. Two years into my PhD research, I finished my neurophysiology qualifying exams. I worked on my dissertation project, and I gathered high-quality data. I purchased a small, lovely studio apartment in downtown Manhattan with high ceilings, and a marble facade, within walking distance of NYU. In a pre-9/11 world, New York City glittered.

My PhD advisor called a lab meeting, and I sat at a big round table with all the other young adults in my lab, thinking we would discuss a paper or an upcoming conference. Then he dropped the bomb and said:

"I'm moving the lab to Oregon. Who is coming, and who is staying?"

After sixty seconds of shock, my head spun. What about my apartment? What about the equipment I built? What about my friends? What about my experiments? I knew within the next sixty seconds—no way I would move to Oregon for the next two to four years of my life.

My lab did move, and the next four years of my life were an unintended exercise in hybrid work. I kept my apartment in NYC. I moved all my equipment to Oregon, losing a year of time in the process. I invested in a high-quality laptop and external drive for data (yes, I had to get a big heavy external drive to plug into my laptop). I bought a fancy cell phone (circa 2000). I did what all PhD students do—I made it work.

I traveled to Oregon for one to six month periods of time to complete experiments with my lab. Then I took my data back home to NYC to analyze and create text and figures by myself. When it came time to write my dissertation, a traditionally lonely exercise, I wrote in many different places—Oregon, NYC, Pennsylvania (visiting family), London (visiting a boyfriend), and the Delaware beach (during a respite from post-9/11 NY).

During these entirely unplanned four years, my hybrid work was enjoyable and surprisingly productive. Without knowing it, I had implemented concepts of deep work and time chunking in a time when online collaboration tools were almost nonexistent.

The concept of deep work is outlined in great depth by Cal Newport in his book with the same title (Newport 2016). There are many examples of great thinkers and artists throughout history who have squirreled themselves away for discrete periods of time to do deep thinking. Examples of authors using deep work include Carl Jung (living in a cabin), or more recently Adam Grant (takes a semester off teaching to write).

During these periods of time, the thinker removed distractions, physical and digital. They intensely focused on one thing—writing, art, research, or other endeavors. When the period of time was over, the thinker stopped doing deep work and returned to other tasks and responsibilities. For Carl Jung, this meant returning to seeing patients, speaking events, and scientific gatherings. For Adam Grant, this meant returning to teaching classes, managing email and social media, and all the other tasks of a successful professor.

Most thinkers required a balance to their solitary, intense, deep work episodes. The balance often came in the form of social events and interactions with people from a variety of backgrounds.

Scientists are a good example of a group of people who have been doing **distributed work** for centuries. A scientist would often spend time alone or with a small team, doing experiments, checking facts, reading other papers, writing. Scientific conferences punctuated lab time. At conferences, scientists gathered in small or large numbers to share findings, debated research, and collided with other scientists in the hallways, meeting rooms, poster displays, speaker sessions, vendor tables, etc. (Gewin 2019).

As I write this chapter, I am doing deep work on an airplane. I have left my wi-fi distractions behind to spend a dedicated two hours of writing time. Tomorrow morning, I will be attending the annual scientific meeting of the American Psychiatric Association where I will present on a debated topic with two colleagues from North Carolina to a room of psychiatrists, nurse practitioners, and other clinicians and researchers from across the country and the globe. I am 100 percent confident tomorrow I will be intellectually stimulated. I will have random and unexpected collisions with old friends and new people. After the meeting tomorrow, I will return home for another period of deep work. I am not alone; scientists and others did this type of distributed work for centuries.

Business leaders also have been doing a variation of time chunking for years. Corporate retreats are a way for leaders to do intense work together and increase collisions with their peers outside of the daily distractions of running an organization (Forbes 2016). Like scientists, academics attend conferences where they are free from their day-to-day responsibilities and periods of deep work in their field of study (Conference2Go 2022).

Our organizations today should stop asking, "should we be in person versus virtual?" We should refocus on how to create intense periods of individual deep work to think, broken by other time chunks of more social and collision-based work. Cal Newport illustrates three different examples. He calls these different schedules *depth philosophies of deep work scheduling*:

The monastic philosophy—We spend most of our time in deep work by radically minimizing the shallow obligations.

- **The bimodal philosophy**—We spend large discrete chunks of time in deep work, alternating with periods of shallow work.
- **The rhythmic philosophy**—We create a daily or weekly rhythm for this work which removes the need to invest energy in deciding if and when we're going deep.
- **The journalistic philosophy**—Like a journalist in the field, we grab your deep work time when we feel the urge, get our thoughts while they are *hot off the press.*

Obviously, the Monastic Philosophy will challenge most people. The other three philosophies are all possibilities, and we can choose which works best at the moment. Personally, I like the rhythmic philosophy. As an example, I wrote 80 percent of this book during discrete chunks of time in my workweek.

Time chunking and minimizing distractions to do deep work resonates with how the human brain functions. Human attention spans appeared shorter as our speed of communication was faster. As someone born before 1985, I experienced this firsthand. As a teenager, it was easy for me to read a 300-page novel in a week. Now, I find it difficult to read anything longer than four pages long.

The type of attention required to read a novel is Sustained Attention. Most neuroscientists agree that there are multiple types of attention which we can categorize into four varieties:

- **Sustained attention**
- **Selective attention**
- **Alternating attention**
- **Divided attention**

I need **sustained attention** to read the 300-page book for hours at a stretch. I need **selective attention** to focus on the words on the page rather than the sound of my dog barking, the cold draft coming through my window, or the thoughts of what I will eat for dinner. In other words, I need selective attention to *stop* attending to stimuli that are unimportant to the task at hand.

MULTITASKING IS A MYTH

In past jobs, my work was full of multitasking. I sat down in the morning with my coffee in hand and looked at my email. I deleted a few emails, drafted a few responses, sent a few answers, and left the rest there for later in the day, incomplete. Then I moved on to a meeting for thirty minutes, where I made a few decisions and left a few for later. I moved on to working on a presentation for ten minutes before I returned to look at email again. I repeated this type of back and forth the entire workday.

This is called **alternating attention** and it is wildly inefficient. Research shows going back and forth between a variety of tasks—**context shifting**—throughout the day without closing out any of the tasks, decreases productivity (MacKay 2021).

According to psychologist Gerald Weinberg, each extra task or 'context' you switch between eats up 20–80 percent of your overall productivity:

- If you focus on one task at a time—you use 100 percent of your productive time available.
- If you task switch between two tasks at a time—you use 40 percent of your productive time for each task, and *you lose 20 percent lost to context shifting.*
- If you task switch between three tasks at a time—you use 20 percent of your productive time for each task, and *you lose 40 percent to context shifting.*

I imagine many of you are thinking—the example above describes forty minutes between email checks—I am

checking email constantly! And Slack DMs and my phone…
"I must be a master multitasker."

Another word for multitasking is **divided attention**, and it is by far the best way to waste your time at work. For each email you answer within fifteen seconds of arrival, your brain must jump back and forth between tasks. This is called **cognitive shift**—when you make a cognitive shift, it takes extra brain energy to disengage with the task you started, engage with the new task, disengage with the new task, and reengage with the original task.

What is multitasking anyway? Evidence suggests that multi-tasking is a myth (Azor 2020). **Multitasking** can be:

Working on two or more tasks simultaneously

- Switching back and forth from one thing to another
- Performing multiple tasks in rapid succession

When I multitasked, I was not doing my brain and body any favors. Research shows multitasking actually hampers productivity by reducing comprehension, attention, and overall performance. Multitasking feels good in the short term because all novelty creates little bursts of neurochemical release in the brain. In the long term, it is simply exhausting.

One solution to multitasking and decreasing the time spent in divided attention is the **touch it once principle** (Pham 2021). With this principle, I created chunks of time to man-age incoming information so I completed the task before I moved on to the next one.

I applied this principle to my email. To touch it once, I set aside a fixed amount of time to attend to my email—whether it be fifteen, thirty, sixty, or one hundred and twenty minutes. I opened my email and completed the task on every single one. To follow-up, I entered the information into my task planner. If I wanted to send a response later, I composed the response and scheduled the send to a later time. If I wanted to save a document, I downloaded the document.

The key here is for me to empty my email inbox during the time allocated to email. Then I turned off my email and my email notifications until the next allocated time for email. If I was in a time-responsive environment, I shortened the time between email chunks. If I was doing deep work without any interruption, the time between email chunks became one business day.

Bottom line: our human attention is a key to effectiveness and efficiency at work. If our teams are stuck in divided and alternating attention modes and not spending time in sustained and selective attention modes, we will be less productive, exhausted, and inefficient. To fix this problem, it matters less how long we allocate to email or when we spend time in deep work. What matters is using the same principles of deep work, touch it once, and other psychological constructs that work with the human brain. In the big picture, it is important to intentionally plan periods of deep work and periods of in person intense work. This practice will efficiently modulate attention and help human brains stay on task.

When we look backward, successful virtual workplace pioneers made it work because they weren't multitasking in a traditional office. They were spending intense periods of time working by themselves or meeting with others. Decades ago, this was unintentional. However, the practice has stuck and is visible in the legacies of scientific conferences and retreats. Let's take a closer look at how we can learn from retreats and scientific meetings to build a better workplace now.

THE FUTURE WON'T WAIT

When I considered people I know who mastered the art of distributed/virtual/hybrid work prepandemic, I knew I wanted to get Sarah Dayes' perspective. Sarah is the chief client officer at a rapidly growing marketing organization. Her company distributed from day one in 2007. Given the success of her organization, Sarah knew where companies were getting it right and where they were getting it wrong in virtual-first organizations.

"I always felt that virtual was a viable way to work and that there are ways to manage around the challenges and all of that," she said.

Sarah recalled when she first started virtual work. The company had trouble being taken seriously, especially outside of the US. Clients found virtual work highly unusual. They had trouble convincing talent to come and work for them as a virtual-first company. They also had trouble convincing clients they could deliver high-quality work without a company headquarters or in-person location.

She admits at first, working virtually made her feel awkward. Sarah said:

"It's just like anything else that is new—it can feel awkward. You just start to do the new thing, and it becomes the norm. Suppose you think about the first time that you were sitting in a conference room and you had another team on a video screen. That probably felt awkward the first time. Some of these things take repetition, and you have to be willing to do things that might feel a little awkward or uncomfortable."

Over time, Sarah found a variety of tools to help her work with her remote teams. She warned that virtual does not equal culture.

"You have to find other deliberate ways to connect. You don't have opportunities to build human connections like happy hour or a walk at lunch. So you have to deliberate about building a human connection. As an example, I start every weekly team meeting with: 'What is the best thing that's happened to you in the last week personally and professionally?' After working with people virtually for five years, I've heard hundreds of things about their personal life. This practice has helped us create culture," she said.

I asked Sarah, "Can you describe companies who are getting it wrong? What common errors are they making?"

"During the pandemic, a lot of companies liked virtual work because they saw more productivity. I believe they're conflating two things that happened at the same time: virtual work and an increase in productivity. In 2020, work went remote for many people; simultaneously, we were also in the middle of the pandemic and people didn't have anything else to do. Many people overworked or worked extra as a coping mechanism. Productivity went through the roof. Companies that went remote during the pandemic are not aware of what is going to happen in the long term. They are assuming that this productivity push will continue as we come out of the pandemic. What they don't know is that virtual work and productivity may be correlated, but not causal," she said.

Sarah found now, most employees expect to have flexibility in their work schedule. People want the ability to work remotely. However, we can't assume remote/virtual equals **culture**. She said:

"These companies will be in for a rude awakening as more and more companies are remote long term and talent starts to understand what is the *right* kind of virtual culture."

Sarah considered having an in-person work component and finding ways to *hub* people to facilitate in-person gathering to be essential. She recommended having at least one in-person event for all junior staff per year. She also recommended more than one in-person event for the leadership team.

"I would not recommend a company that literally has people all over the place. I think you need to have some sort of a talent geographical strategy," she said.

Employees now expect flexibility at work—a combination of virtual and in-person work. If an organization returns to the traditional office and the traditional nine-to-five way of working together in person, it will dramatically limit its talent pool. It will only hire people who:

- live close enough to the geographic location of the physical office or are willing to relocate
- do not need or do not value flexibility
- people who don't like or prefer to avoid virtual work

LISTENING TO PSYCHOLOGISTS RATHER THAN BUSINESS CONSULTANTS

One of my inspirations to write this book came from my friends and colleagues—whom I greatly respect and value—who told me, "We just want to go back to normal" or "If we are going to work virtually, we should take the advice of business best practices." As much as I respect and value these individuals, I couldn't disagree more.

A decade ago, I saw patients day in and day out. On the other hand, my husband worked as an attorney within a large global corporation, surrounded by businesspeople all day. He would bring home new corporate lingo he heard—words like *optionality, cascading, de-risking,* etc. We laughed together—these words were silly and unnecessary.

Years later, when I worked in a large corporate environment surrounded by businesspeople, it got serious. I had to become a cultural anthropologist to quickly learn the cultures of the business, finance, operations, and sales functions of the organization. I had to learn an entirely new lexicon of business-speak. I didn't understand these terms, and I felt lost in conversations.

As with other types of cultural anthropology, my observations became more nuanced with time. I saw how the business lingo differed for different groups of businesspeople. Eventually, I understood this business lingo descended from the business school my colleagues attended. People who had an MBA from Harvard used slightly different lingo than people who had an MBA from Stanford or Wharton.

As another familiar example—physicians and attorneys have their own tribes and their own lingo foreign to the majority of people. Creating lingo is an entirely normal and predictable human behavior. We all find our tribes, and we all learn the tribal culture. Shared lingo helps us make meaningful connections.

This is important with regard to the workplace because many of the business consultants and the business writers all came from the same tribes. They learned to communicate in their own ways. They had common schemas and assumptions. People with MBAs from prestigious schools worked for prestigious business consulting firms, and they wrote in prestigious business journals. They consulted the same individuals for business best practices.

To understand if a business practice works, we must test it scientifically. We must continually make observations to change course if needed. I observed consultants giving similar advice year after year. Business best practices were outdated and ineffective. Unfortunately, with few people to challenge the business schemas and assumptions, organizations persisted in doing things that did not make sense.

As an example, I saw business consultants state that past performance predicts future performance. The science of probability and statistics tells us this is simply not true. Galton's Law of Regression to the Mean tells us what looks like a positive outlier one year may simply go back to the normal curve the next year due to chance alone (Farnam Street 2020).

The pandemic caught the workplace off guard because most organizations were following "best practices" without being aware of their own schemas and assumptions. We can reconsider our assumptions, and we can bring neuroscience and psychology to the workplace.

We can learn much from psychologists who understand both business and people. Dr. Sabrina Starling is living in the future of work now. She had various career experiences, including working as a community psychotherapist, a virtual psychotherapist, an entrepreneur, a business owner, and an author. Dr. Sabrina considers how humans work best, and her company helps other small businesses design healthy and sustainable workplaces, both for the employees and the business owner.

I knew from Dr. Sabrina's book that she was optimistic for the future of work, saying: "The pandemic created a zeitgeist: there is more to life than work." Dr. Sabrina told me she researched the topic of work for her book *The 4 Week Vacation®* (Starling 2021).

I asked Dr. Sabrina, "What are some tips and tricks for businesses to design more humanistic ways to work?"

"In the first half of the book, I did a really deep dive into all the different research on why shorter work weeks are better.

Working less makes us more effective. The notion that working in an office forty hours a week is outdated. It doesn't fit with our lifestyles. When we give people flexibility and freedom, they will be more engaged in their work, and they will take more ownership," she said.

Dr. Sabrina and her team actually work less. She said:

"When I started my business, I decided I would only work twenty-five hours a week. This was the most time I was willing to put my baby daughter with a babysitter. I just had to make it work. The fun thing I learned about limiting my work time is that it forced me to focus on what is most important. Every day, I asked, 'What's the most important thing I can do right now that will move the business forward?' I focused on getting that one thing done. It allowed me permission to let other things go. Fifteen years later, I continue to use that question to grow my business, and I still work about twenty-five hours a week."

I asked, "How do you manage a team of employees who work less than forty hours per week?"

"I don't want anyone on our team working forty hours a week because I want them to have flexibility. I want them to take care of things at home and with their family. I want them to be doing things outside of work. This time not working adds to who they are. It adds to how they show up to work. It adds to what they bring to our clients. This applies to everyone on our team. I want everyone to have a life away from work," she said.

I knew Dr. Sabrina's team is spread across multiple time zones, working remotely from their homes.

Next, I asked, "What tips and tricks have you learned as a manager to work effectively in a distributed team?"

"Have a clear dedicated space for work and only use that space for work. This can be as simple as a particular chair—that's your work chair, and you only sit there when you're working. Define for yourself what your ideal schedule is.

"Notice when you're most productive for certain tasks and build your schedule around that. Make it clear when you're available and when you're not available. On my team, all of us have to set limits around when we are available.

"Teach people how to communicate with you. For example, just because somebody can text you doesn't mean you have to respond right away. It is okay to be out of pocket. We all need downtime where we are unavailable so that we can show up and be fully present when we are available," she said.

Finally, I asked, "What does your business feel like? Does it feel chaotic to have your employees all working on variable, flexible schedules?"

"If you have expectations around results that need to be delivered, the focus shifts from people working at a certain time. It's really important to clarify the results that you're expecting to be delivered and when you need those delivered but teach your team to set boundaries. One of my colleagues has this beautiful tagline on her email: "Your work hours may be different from my work hours. If you're receiving this at an odd hour, don't feel compelled to respond until it's your work hours." she said.

I saw Dr. Sabrina and her team at work. As a leader, she did more than have clarity around time, communication, and expectations. Likely as a result of her temperament and her training as a psychotherapist, Dr. Sabrina is extraordinarily humanistic. She actively fostered and practiced *judgment-free* zones so her employees felt safe and supported, and the team stayed curious and dug into *failures*.

"It's our human nature to judge what's wrong in our environment. This is how we are hardwired," she said.

Leaders and managers have to proactively manage the work environment to bring out the best in people.

I can imagine what it would be like to work with Dr. Sabrina, where I have flexibility and autonomy and feel appreciated in a deeply humanistic way. I can imagine what it would be like to work with Sarah Dayes and her distributed team with her in-person events. I can imagine what it will feel like to plan my next in-person work event and what it will feel like when I am back home, doing deep work in a way that makes the most efficient use of my time and my brain. I can imagine the future of work now.

SUMMARY
Hybrid and virtual work existed for centuries—we didn't see it because of the dominance of the traditional office.

Scientific meetings, academic conferences, and leadership retreats are a few examples. People have been making it work and exceeding expectations for years.

The pandemic accelerated existing trends to work outside of the traditional office. Best practices of the past are simply not the best practices of today. Organizations can design their workplace with input from psychologists, with the goal of bringing more humanism to work. On the other hand, just because a company works virtually, it does not automatically make it productive, nor does it equal strong culture. Virtual does not equal humanistic, and organizations that work virtually without attention to how humans work best will suffer the same fate as the traditional office.

I hope this chapter highlights the key elements of a humanistic workplace.

Alternating intense periods of deep work individually or on small teams with short bursts of in-person work may work best. Minimizing distraction and keeping attention in one place are keys to this strategy. Creating and fostering an environment of curiosity and learning, not judging, can help to make people feel safe and valued at work. Flexible and autonomous work means the elimination of face time and a shift to other measurements of success.

In the next chapter, I paint the picture of what it looks like when people thrive in virtual and hybrid work. What can work look like right now?

CHAPTER 14

How to Make Work Not Suck

———

Building a workplace that does not suck requires foundational building blocks of time management, communication, and empathy.

Spoiler alert: the same ideas apply to in person and virtual work. They may be easier to apply to virtual work because old (human) habits are hard to break in person.

Being a better human at work doesn't require mastering time perfectly, communicating perfectly, or being perfectly empathetic. You can infuse humanism at work by increasing your self-awareness. After awareness comes intention, and after intention comes practice and iteration.

BABY STEPS—OBSERVATION AND AWARENESS

In the fall of 1982, I loved fourth grade. For years, I played school with my stuffed animals (and occasionally my reluctant little sister). I always sat in the front of the class-room and eagerly raised my hand. It felt good to know the answer.

As a nine-year-old, my awareness of other people increased. I realized that not everyone raised their hand. My classmates clearly knew the answer but didn't raise their hands. Why?

I am embarrassed to admit that this pattern persisted for another fifteen years without much self-awareness. I continued to raise my hand, regardless of the situation. I was oblivious to other people around me who had something to say.

Things shifted in medical school when I didn't know all the answers. I stopped raising my hand. I stopped talking and started listening. I listened carefully to others in my classes because I needed to learn from them. I realized I was not a good listener for the last twenty years in school. I was too busy raising my hand to talk.

Fast forward another fifteen years, and I found myself right back to wanting to be the kid who knew all the answers. Whenever I started a new job, I wanted to add value to the conversation. I didn't listen well. I missed out on what others had to say.

Luckily, I became self-aware. I checked myself, and I relearned how to listen through awareness of my own personal tendencies. As I worked virtually, I got much better at observing myself, holding back, and resisting the urge to jump in and add value. The in-person setting stimulated me. I struggled to resist the energy in the room.

I found ways to check myself. I continue to practice and fight my tendencies. In virtual settings, I put myself on mute. I draft communications and do not hit send right away. In-person settings, I set intentions before the day starts to listen actively. I write this down on my top three tasks for the day. I still fight the desire to raise my hand, and I see myself fighting it. However, I know observation and intention are half the battle.

There is an entire scientific discipline based on the idea of observation and intention in the workplace—**industrial and organizational (I/O) psychology.** I/O psychologists study and assess individual, group, and organizational dynamics in the workplace. They apply I/O research to identify solutions to improve the well-being and performance of organizations and their employees.

You can learn and use the same tools I/O psychologists use on a smaller scale. These tools help make meaningful changes now to teams and organizations. My story above was an example of how I applied the concepts of I/O psychology at work.

We can explain I/O psychology in five steps, which loop one through five, then repeat:

- **Observation**—What do you see in your workplace and in yourself at work?
- **Hypothesis generation**—Based on your observations and other background research, what is your theory about what is happening?

- **Hypothesis testing**—What experiment can you do in your workplace to test the hypothesis?
- **Conclusions**—After doing the experiment, what conclusions can you draw?
- **Application**—How can you apply your conclusions?

Let's start with a specific example of I/O psychology at work:

Observation—I feel like work sucks. I observed myself one week at work. I notice days when I am on video all day, I feel grumpy and tired at dinner, and the one day I wasn't on video, I felt good.

- **Hypothesis generation**—I do online research and find research that supports the idea that video calls increase fatigue. I create a hypothesis—my work sucks because I am on video all day long.
- **Hypothesis testing**—I can get feedback from my team on video meetings with a simple poll. This is quantitative data because it can generate numbers. This is an open ended question qualitative data because it asks people how they feel.
- **Conclusions**—Based on my simple poll, 50 percent of people said they didn't like video meetings, 25 percent said they liked them, and 25 percent said they were neutral. I concluded that if we cut back on the number of video meetings, most people would feel better, and work would suck less. The free responses said work would be significantly better if they were not on video so frequently because it made them tired at the end of the day.
- **Application**—I tell my team we are going to do an experiment, and we are going to decrease our video meetings

to 50 percent for the next two weeks, and I am going to ask for their feedback at the end of those two weeks. We do the experiment, and I ask for feedback at the end of the two weeks.

- **Observation**—I loop back to step one. I observe that I personally feel like work sucks less. I observe that most people on the team are slightly more productive, and a few people on the team are less productive. I share my observations in a team meeting, and we repeat the cycle. This time I decreased video meetings to 25 percent and spent extra one-on-one time with the few people who were less productive to see what happened with them.

You may be thinking this is so slow. It would take forever if I made a small change every two weeks.

Make no mistake, you will likely feel tempted to skip steps and make multiple changes at the same time. You might go through steps one through five and forget to loop back to the beginning. These are all common human tendencies. Even scientists take years of practice to master this technique.

When other people start seeing results, even small ones, they will want to try this method themselves. You can build trust through feedback loops and transparency. You might also identify a few people in your team who tend to get their way because they are persuasive or vocal (see my example of raising my hand all the time). Gathering data from the entire group can help you avoid listening to people raising their hands all the time.

SETTING YOUR INTENTION AND GETTING RESULTS

Several years ago, I had the privilege to work with a distinguished physician who rose through the ranks of his healthcare organization. Due to corporate restructuring, he ended up reporting to me, even though I was twenty years his junior.

On the surface, this physician had humanism nailed. Deeply kind and compassionate to his patients, all the other members of his direct team respected him. He was quiet, a good listener, communicated well, and didn't rush. Despite these foundational leadership skills, he still felt like work sucked (note—this is my terminology, he would never say work sucked).

This senior leader was puzzled and frustrated by the failure of other clinicians to do the right thing. He didn't understand why they weren't performing up to their abilities. He didn't understand why his attempts to correct their behavior failed. He couldn't make the change he wanted, and this reflected poorly on him as a leader.

As we worked together, I introduced the concepts described earlier in this book—how to identify biases and schemas and how to challenge assumptions. We did group exercises with other leaders to open up thinking and improve empathy for their teams. After a few months, I saw something click for this leader. He focused less on data and outcomes and more on the people on his team. He got curious and set an intention to inject more humanism into his work.

Once he set this intention, work flowed. Being skilled at listening, compassion, and communication with his patients, he switched gears and applied the same skills to his team of clinicians. He acted like an I/O psychologist. He did small experiments with his team. I helped him plan his experiments, and we debriefed on what succeeded and failed. He felt energized. Work no longer sucked.

As a coach and a psychotherapist, I see people gradually increase their own self-awareness, set intentions, then act on them in a curious and nonjudgmental manner. Over time, they internalize the dialog you have together. Eventually, they don't need you anymore because they do the work on their own. One of my recent clients joked with me that she wanted a T-shirt with *What would Jennie say?* on it as a reminder to continue this self-dialog. The key to making the intention to be a better human at work is follow-through. If you set the intention without the observation and the experimenting, it doesn't stick. It is too rational. It is not real. Some people make this process look effortless.

When I thought about people who are amazing human beings at work, both virtually and in person, I thought of Nina Perales. Nina trained as a psychotherapist. Her work included a variety of in person and virtual settings, doing patient care, creating programs and systems, and helping others understand the importance of psychological safety. Working with Nina, I felt understood. She fostered humanism at work by creating safe spaces and improving extraordinarily complicated team dynamics. She was comfortable with uncomfortable situations, sharing emotions, and sitting silently with others.

I asked Nina what it was like to work with a new team in a virtual setting with occasional touch-points. She told me she didn't love working 100 percent virtually as a therapist. However, she really enjoys working with her new distributed team. She said:

"I think working virtually does help to give a safer workspace. It gives more space for having privacy with conversations and with observations. When you can just turn off a meeting at the end, that's safe for the people to feel like they can address difficult things."

"It is so much easier to deal with difficult, annoying, or disastrous meetings working at home. Recently I had a virtual meeting with a colleague who was in the office. She was late to a phone call, and she said, 'I'm so sorry. I just want to apologize because I know you're working from home and you're by yourself and you're just sitting here waiting on this call'.

"I responded, 'Thank you, and probably pre-COVID-19, that's how I would have felt. Now I feel bad for you because when my meeting is over, I don't have to walk back to my desk with somebody and look at them still and try to figure out how to get space from them. I can just click off, and go play with my dogs or go outside at my own house. I can break from the situation. I don't have to be around it,'" she said.

I asked her what she saw with team dynamics in the remote setting. I wanted to know if people were doing better or worse managing interpersonal team dynamics in the virtual workspace?

"Working virtually, the relational dynamics [of the team]—both good and bad—are spotlighted so much more. You can't just overlook them.

"For example, when a policy gets created, there is often tension. It is usually because there was a bad thing that happened for the policy to get created in the first place. We recently had a situation working remotely where a policy had to be put in place due to the actions of one of the people on the team. After the creation of the policy, there was still a lot of unspoken discomfort among the team. From a therapist's perspective, I knew that processing hadn't fully happened to allow closure for the team.

"So, when it was time to announce the new policy at the staff meeting, I actually broke down and cried. I said this was a policy that needed to happen, that it was unintentionally and unfortunately at the expense of one of our team members. And I wanted to extend an apology to that person. I wanted to give gratitude for their work. I wanted to acknowledge how hard it has been on that person and others on their team.

"I also knew that if it hadn't acknowledged it at that level, if I didn't say something, it would never have been properly addressed. The policy would have just felt like a top-down decision that was not genuine," she said.

I asked her what would have happened if she had not been there. She felt there would have been no closure on the human element of the situation, and this would have created distrust among the team. By calling out the discomfort, showing emotion, and demonstrating empathy, Nina used a negative situation to build trust among the team.

In the virtual setting, we often forget human dynamics. We often forget to speak of the human element in a bad situation. Nina showed how intentional humanism in the virtual workplace can actually bond people together and deepen trust.

I imagine after that difficult call, a virtual team member shut their laptop, took deep breaths, and went out for a short walk. They processed the human aspect of what happened without being overwhelmed. They took actions to reduce their own emotional state in a safe space.

In the traditional office, taking a pause from an intense team moment would have been much more difficult. I imagine even Nina would have struggled to demonstrate that level of humanism in the in-person setting. The scenario would have been intense, and it would be difficult for the team to move on and go back to work surrounded by emotion. In Nina's words: "Virtual work gives a safer space for observations and conversations."

Nina's story exemplified creating safe spaces and sensitivity to human dynamics. As part of writing this book, I researched how we can create safe spaces at work. What I found surprised me. Most of the research discussed being *politically correct* (circa 1990s), or *woke* (circa 2000s), or how to avoid saying anything which might offend or *trigger* (circa 2010s) anyone in the workplace.

I fundamentally disagree with the idea that creating a safe workspace means avoiding conflict by neutralizing our language and our actions. Based on my experience as a psychiatrist, a psychotherapist, and a leader, I believe the opposite. Creating a truly safe and humanistic workplace has to do with how humans manage conflict, not how they remove all potentially conflict-filled situations.

MANAGING CONFLICT AT WORK

Conflict is a normal and healthy part of being a human. Work can improve when we understand the different styles of **conflict management**. If we shift to healthier ways of managing conflict, we will be better humans at work. Our workplace will be more humanistic and suck less.

One framework to understand the psychology of human conflict management is the Thomas-Kilmann Conflict Mode Instrument (TKI), used by HR professionals around the world since 1974 (Kilmann 2020). In this framework, there are five major styles of conflict management:

Collaborative conflict—The *healthiest* way to manage conflict—it is a curious, nonjudgmental way to collaborate around the conflict and come to solutions.

- **Competitive conflict**—Conflict is experienced as a competition—to be the winner you need to win the conflict.
- **Avoidant conflict**—This is by far the most common way to manage conflict—you avoid it.

- **Accommodating conflict**—You manage conflict by giving in and letting the other person get their way, aka you are the *martyr*.
- **Compromising conflict**—You agree to disagree and come to a practical compromise in the conflict.

To create safe workspaces where you can have healthy conflict, you want to maximize the amount of **collaborative conflict** and minimize the other types of conflict at work. In her best-selling book, *Radical Candor*, Kim Scott discussed the value of conflict at work (Scott 2019). She described how to engage in productive conflict while at the same time showing you deeply care about the individual(s) who you are in conflict with. One of her key takeaways from *Radical Candor* was the feedback loop—you must use active listening and continually give, solicit, and receive feedback.

Another framework to create safe spaces for conflict resolution is popular with psychotherapists—the STABEN method. STABEN gives you a way to plan and execute simple assertive conflict discussions which are efficient and effective (Staben 2022). STABEN stands for:

- **S—Source**
- **T—Time and place**
- **A—Amicable approach**
- **B—Behavior**
- **E—Emotion**
- **N—Need**

My favorite example of using STABEN comes from doing the dishes. Here is how I would use STABEN to approach a conflict situation with my husband in which I am doing the dishes too frequently:

S—**Source**—in this story, the source of the conflict is my husband.

- **T—Time and place**—I select Sunday morning after breakfast to have this conversation because I know both of us will have rested, and we don't have any other immediate plans. I plan to talk to him at the table.
- **A—Amicable approach**—I start by pointing out one thing I am genuinely grateful for "I really appreciate you made breakfast this morning—it was thoughtful."
- **B—Behavior**—I identify the behavior I observe. "I have noticed that last week you did the dishes after dinner only one time, even though we agreed to split this task fifty-fifty."
- **E—Emotion**—I identify the emotion I felt. "This makes me feel unappreciated."
- **N—Need**—I clearly say what I need. "I need you to follow through on doing the dishes 50 percent of the time without me asking you first."

I know STABEN works because I have used it myself. I have trained hundreds of patients to use it. I made a video describing this technique which has thousands of views on YouTube with multiple requests to use the video in a variety of workplace trainings (Byrne 2013). Most people worry they are too passive (avoiding, compromising, or accommodating) or too aggressive (competing). They need simple tools to help them be more assertive (Collaborating). Assertiveness and collaboration build stronger relationships, if relationships can tolerate and manage their conflict, the workspace will create space for humanism to thrive.

Whichever framework resonates with you, the key is to get moving and try things. You don't need to be a therapist or an HR leader to create safe spaces and humanism in your workplace.

CHAPTER 15

The Big Question

———

The thing that differentiates companies and organizations is how human they are.

—Indra Nooyi (Nooyi 2021)

Traditional work sucked. A new focus on humanism and human connectedness can revolutionize how we view work. The future of work has far-reaching implications for humanity and our planet.

HUMANISM IS THE FUTURE OF WORK

Like most teenagers, I experienced difficulty fitting in. In the summer of seventh grade, I truly fit in for the first time. In the middle of a hot 1985 summer, I attended Franklin and Marshall College in Lancaster, Pennsylvania, for a boarding summer program run by Johns Hopkins CTY, aka *nerd camp*.

I spent the next three weeks living in a college dorm with a roommate and hall-mates, attending archaeology classes during the day. In the evening, we played games, danced, and studied together. We took a field trip to an actual archaeology dig site where I sweat buckets through my favorite Esprit teal T-shirt. I spent hours sifting dirt, rewarded by an arrowhead at the end of the day.

We ate all our meals together. We slept in the same dorms together. We attended classes together. I loved it. We shared experiences, both academic and social. I never felt more in sync with a group of people than I did that summer.

When you are in sync with another person or a group of people, it feels different. At CTY, I experienced a deep sense of human connectedness. For me, this has only occurred a few times. I continue to seek out this experience of human connectedness both in my personal life and at work. When I find connectedness at work with a client or a colleague, my work feels meaningful, in large part because it expresses humanism.

This sense of human connectedness happens when I am physically together with people at work. It happens virtually when we create things together. It happens when I help a leader create a culture for their team. I find it difficult to articulate this feeling of connectedness and even more difficult to make it concrete and give examples that are easy for others to replicate.

Indra Nooyi speaks out for the need for humanism in the future of work. In 2006, PepsiCo appointed her as CEO, making her one of the most powerful women in business. Born in Chennai, India, Indra spoke about the importance of her cultural background in shaping her approach to business.

In a speech at Georgetown, she said:

"The world is becoming so borderless and so global, and the thing that differentiates companies and organizations is how human they are" (Nooyi 2021).

In a recent interview, Adam Grant asked Indra why people considered her a leader who deeply cared for her employees despite her communication style of being blunt and honest. Indra Nooyi told Adam the story of how she worked as an executive at Pepsi and traveled home to visit her family in India. Her parents sat her on the couch and people visited. They said hello to Indra, and they spent time with her parents. They told them what a good job they did as parents and how they were so proud of Indra and how she represented the family, the community, and the country (Nooyi 2021).

This experience led her to realize the importance of work on other people in the family and the community. She saw the importance of her work firsthand. Her family and her family's community found her work meaningful. They felt a sense of pride in how her parents raised her and the values which she took from her community and spread around the world. Her family and her community shared in her sense of meaning and success.

Based on this experience, Indra thought of ways to add non-monetary value to her executives who were high performers. She decided to handwrite thoughtful letters to the parents of the executives, including 1) context of why she wrote this letter, 2) specific details concerning the executive's meaningful work, and 3) her thanks to the parents for the good work they did raising the exec and thanks for sharing their talent with her. She received an emotional and mind-blowing response, so she continued this practice over the years. She wrote hundreds of letters to the parents and spouses of her top talent.

She concluded the interview by saying she wants the future of work conversation to stop focusing exclusively on tech, communication, and offices. She wants the conversation to focus on how we will start infusing humanism into the future of work.

Humanism is a philosophy that emphasizes the value of human beings. Based on the belief that humans are capable of rational thought and self-reflection, humanism encourages people to think for themselves and to make decisions based on reason and empathy. This approach allows people to lead meaningful and fulfilling lives.

Humanism dates back to the fifteenth century. Since then, humanism has evolved into a variety of different movements, including liberalism, human rights activism, and feminism.

There are a number of ways businesses can embrace humanism in the workplace:

- They can focus on the needs of employees—offering flexible working arrangements, and providing training and development opportunities.
- They can focus on customer service—create a positive customer experience, ensuring their customers feel valued and respected.

- They can promote ethical values—honesty, integrity, and social responsibility.

Indra's story highlighted several psychologically savvy tools in a simple and easy-to-understand and implement format.

Artifacts—Handwritten letters show you are taking the time to write. They are also a physical artifact. Physical artifacts help build strong teams. These types of rewards which are tangible, are more powerful than abstract rewards.

Offering context—Indra knew her parents would worry about getting a letter from her and immediately jump to the wrong conclusion. By offering context, she showed empathy and a deep understanding of the letter recipient.

Personalization—She gave specific examples in her feedback to show she observed, listened, and reflected. Feeling heard means people feel valued.

Offering pride—Indra gave the parents a feeling of pride which had a high emotional impact on both the parent and the exec. This feeling of pride had a huge value and cost nothing.

Saying thank you—Indra showed she understands the exec is a whole person and they have a life outside of work. She recognizes there were likely times the exec had to choose work over a family request. She knew the value of the executive's time and energy. She showed a deep understanding of what it means to the family to have their child working as an exec, both the good and the bad.

Extending the thanks—When Indra wrote a letter to a spouse, she showed all the same benefits above. However, the letter to the spouse has the added benefit of loyalty. If the spouse feels heard and understood, they are much more likely to support the exec when they need to spend time and energy at work. When the work gets tough, the executive might be more likely to stay on the job.

Indra's solution was so simple, so elegant, and so easy to execute with maximal impact. If we create solutions like these, we will infuse humanism into the future of work.

Indra Nooyi demonstrated the power of understanding a simple tenet—humans are hardwired for social connections (Penttila 2019). During the pandemic, we all experienced detachment from social connections. For many people, this created profound discomfort, depression, and anxiety.

GETTING IN SYNC

The idea of being "in sync" with another person comes from the idea of synchrony. **Synchrony** is *a simultaneous action, development, or occurrence.* When we think about synchrony, we often think about music playing or athletes moving in synchrony.

Synchronous sounds, movement, or other stimuli are pleasing to humans. Human brains have electrical activity which synchronizes to different rhythms. Neuroscience research suggests the way we put together all the pieces of a stimulus (sound, smell, and feeling) is through simultaneous firing (electrical discharges) of brain cells.

In other words, for us to experience a moment in time or for us to recall a memory, we need synchrony of neuronal activity in the brain. This happens on a millisecond scale. We are typically not conscious of this happening in our brains. As you read these words, different parts of your brain synchronize to connect the visual images with the word meanings and connect to other schemas, memories, or ideas in your brain.

When we are *in sync* with other people, we are literally synchronized with them at a neuronal level. When we listen to music together, we are linking the activity of our brains together. When we feel connected to other people, the patterns of our brain activity connect. When two people experience empathy, their brain waves flow in similar patterns. Even more interesting, when teams of people play a video game together and experience a flow state, their brain activity synchronizes.

In the future of work, finding ways to flow, connect, and synchronize with other humans happens in person or virtually. An AI cannot replicate this human experience at least not at the time of writing this book. However, technology and AI help remove much of the need for human labor, leaving us with the time and energy to focus more on developing more humanism in the workplace.

The future of work includes tech. AI will work as *helpers*, taking on the manual or overtly rational tasks that robots are good at. Humans will be able to work on connectedness, creativity, and other meaningful activities. We desire manual labor and rational work as human tasks because we struggle to imagine what would happen if AI replaced human labor.

THE ELEPHANT IN THE ROOM—IF AI REPLACES HUMAN LABOR, WHAT NEXT?

At the time of writing this book, I am helping a start-up organization select a group of technological tools to enable our work. We are deciding what tech tools the organization will use and how we will use these tools.

As part of these decisions, I get caught up in debates concerning which tech tool or suite of tools is better. I get pulled into all the gadgets and gizmos of the tech tools. I get emotional about which tools I like better and which ones I hate. I think of old memories of my past experiences working with tech and AI. I too make assumptions, and I am biased.

I find it difficult to step back and ask: *What are the things we are trying to get humans to do or not to do?* We feel tempted to replace the tech tools with more in-person time because we assume returning to in-person work will be a magical solution. I believe we are missing the point.

The real question is—how does the tech make the culture better?

The tech should enable everything discussed earlier in the book—time management, communication, and empathy. Our tech should support us so we can focus on infusing more humanism into the workplace. If we distract ourselves with debates concerning our favorite tech tool, we avoid this more difficult question concerning culture and humanism.

We can dig deeper. If our tech tools are better at our work, humans will have less work to do. If humans have less work to do, we will have more free time.

Naturally, we might fill our new free time with new tasks or busywork. We might fill our free time with emails and DMs. Our culture remains a culture that celebrates busyness, long to-do lists, and checking off boxes. Most of us are comfortable with the idea that humans can have meaningful lives while simultaneously working less, having fewer to-do lists, and fewer boxes to check off.

In reality, the future of work has already arrived. AI has already taken over many human tasks, and you probably haven't even noticed.

For example, look at ride services like Uber and Lyft. These services operate on a tech platform that takes many of the steps traditionally associated with a taxi driver. The AI schedules a pickup, navigates to a destination, gives approximate travel times, takes payment, and solicits feedback. Other than physically driving the car (which AI will soon take over as well), what are the human Uber and Lyft drivers actually doing?

The drivers spend their time and energy making the ride a better experience for you as a human passenger. They spend time and energy ensuring their cars are clean and smell good. They spend time and energy being on timely pick-ups. They chat with you during the ride and bring positive energy to your day. They do all these things because they are no longer in the business of being a taxi driver. They are in the business of being empathetic to their passengers, attending to your needs, and anticipating what you think is important. The drivers make a human connection with you during the ride.

They do these things because in the model of Uber and Lyft, humanism is incentivized. When you give a driver a five-star rating, it matters. If a driver is a bad human on a given day, not empathetic to your needs, with a bad attitude, or late arrival, you are likely to give them four-, three-, two-, or one-star rating. The more negative reviews they get, the more they will get rejected by future passengers. Uber has a program called Uber Pro, where drivers are rewarded by higher star ratings with different types of financial and logistic rewards (Uber Pro 2022).

When you incentivize good human behavior with the right incentives, it works.

In the world of healthcare, we are starting to add financial incentives for physicians to be better humans at work. Healthcare faces an explosion of tech and AI. Physicians find themselves in uncomfortable situations where AI is better at a traditionally human physician task. For example, in a 2020 Nature article, AI detected breast cancers on mammograms more accurately than human radiologists (McKinney 2020).

Physicians, like Uber and Lyft drivers, should welcome AI helpers at work. Having AI take on human labor and rational algorithms frees up physicians to be better humans and to make deeper connections with their patients. At the end of the day, people value the human connection with their physician as much as the physician's technical abilities.

Bedside manner matters. Healing happens when you have a deep human connection of trust and mutual caring with your health care providers. Healthcare payers think bedside manner matters too, and they are willing to financially incentive it. Patient satisfaction surveys are gaining traction in the five-star rating system for Medicare Advantage health plans. In these plans, health providers receive bonus money when their patients report a good experience, similar to Uber and Lyft drivers.

Long term, AI will take on more and more helper tasks for humans. We can focus more on being better humans and fostering humanism at work. What happens next? Let's imagine our experience in the more distant future when we are freed from traditional work.

THE BIG QUESTION—WHAT IF WE DON'T NEED TO WORK

The years 1991, 1995, 2004, 2006, and 2021 all had one thing in common for me. I had brief periods of being between jobs or not working due to a planned transition or a surprise. Fortunately, I supported myself during these times, whether through savings or debt. I paid the bills and avoided financial hardship.

Despite being financially stable, *each time I was not doing traditional work, I felt profoundly uncomfortable.* Generally speaking, not doing traditional work feels negative in our culture. There were plenty of societal messages telling me I failed because I didn't go to a traditional office forty hours a week.

I felt ungrounded without a clear work identity. The idea of leisure did not attract me. My restless brain needed challenging, or it would turn inward, and I would become extremely anxious. So, during these periods of time, I took online courses and found things to keep my brain active while I rebuilt my social network.

These breaks from work made me think: *What would it be like in the future when we give up our culture of busyness and the need always to be working?*

Daniel Susskind tackled this big question. Daniel trained as a classic economist, then investigated the intersection of technology and economics. He currently works as a research professor in Economy at King's College in London. He is also the author of *A World Without Work* (Susskind 2020).

As the COVID-19 pandemic erupted, Daniel started asking big questions (Russell 2021). He asked:

"The final challenge we will face in a world with less work, I argue, is finding meaning in life. If employment dries up, where will that sense of direction come from?"

Based on his research, he came to three conclusions.

- The pandemic requires entirely new types of intervention.

- The challenges we face are global.
- While the challenges are immense, there are important opportunities in how we choose to respond.

Daniel joined his colleague Stuart Russell in a meeting with other thought leaders to discuss the future of work in November 2021. The group included Madeline Ashby (science fiction author and expert in strategic foresight), Ken Liu (Hugo Award-winning science fiction and fantasy author), and economists Daron Acemoglu (MIT) and Anna Salomons (Utrecht), among many others.

Daniel was surprised by the amount of disagreement amongst the group members. The group conversation turned quickly to values. They debated what defines a good society. They couldn't agree on what a good balance between work and life looked like.

Two camps of thought emerged from the meeting:

1. "Freed from the shackles of traditional work, humans could use their new freedom to engage in exploration, self-improvement, volunteering, or whatever else they find satisfying."
2. "Traditional work might still be essential... People will engage in supplying interpersonal services which we can provide—or which we prefer to provide—only by humans. These include therapy, tutoring, life coaching, and community-building. If we can no longer supply routine physical labor and routine mental labor, we can still supply our humanity."

A BRIGHTER TOMORROW

After much debate, the group did not agree on a single vision of the future. However, they did agree on six key components of an optimistic future of work.

Key Component #1—Shared economic prosperity

People around the world widely share the economic benefits of technological progress. The global economy is ten times larger because AI has massively boosted productivity. Humans can do more and achieve more by sharing this prosperity. We can pursue this vision by adopting various interventions, from introducing a global tax regime to improving insurance against unemployment.

A more equitable distribution of wealth in the future is highly attractive. Access to information and education is more distributed due to smartphones and internet access. In theory, AI can level the playing field. If we no longer rely on geographic- or language- or skill-based work skills as *tokens* to trade for wealth, in theory, we have an opportunity to distribute wealth in a more creative and equitable manner.

Key Component #2—Realigned companies

Large companies focus on developing AI that benefits humanity and they do so without holding excessive economic or political power. Changing corporate ownership structures and updating antitrust policies is a way to pursue this.

This opportunity exists today. Leaders in companies can make smarter purchasing decisions regarding technology and AI, which works with the human brain and behavior rather than against it. For example, companies can invest in psychologically sound performance management AI systems that understand how to impact employee behavior positively.

Key Component #3—Flexible labor markets

Human creativity and hands-on support give people time to find new roles. People adapt to technological change and find work in newly created professions. Policies would focus on improving educational and retraining opportunities, as well as strengthening social safety nets for those who would otherwise be worse off due to automation.

In our culture, people strongly identify with their work and leaving work can be quite jarring to one's self-image. A brighter future of work must also reframe our identity. We can increase our level of curiosity and play. We can help adults enter ongoing education mindsets so they are always retraining and learning.

Key Component #4—Human-centric AI

Society decides against excessive automation. Business leaders, computer scientists, and policymakers choose to develop technologies that increase rather than decrease the demand for workers. Incentives to develop human-centric AI would strengthen and automation taxed where necessary.

Some organizations already follow this strategy. They look to technology and AI to increase productivity and decrease the demand for workers. I saw successful teams which had redundancy within their staff. In other words, there are extra humans on the team, so when vacation, illness, or life happens, there are others on the team who can pick up the work without feeling burdened.

Key Component #5—Fulfilling jobs

New jobs are more fulfilling than those which came before. Machines handle unsafe and boring tasks, while humans move into more productive, fulfilling, and flexible jobs with greater human interaction. Policies to achieve this include strengthening labor unions and increasing worker involvement on corporate boards.

We can all make steps toward more fulfilling and flexible jobs with greater human interaction. The pandemic created a real sense of possibility at both ends of the spectrum. We consider what it would feel like to do fulfilling and flexible work. We also saw what happens when we do neither fulfilling nor flexible work. The Great Resignation of people shifting jobs highlighted this movement toward more fulfilling and more flexible jobs.

Key Component #6—Civic empowerment and human flourishing

In a world with less need to work and basic needs met by UBI, well-being increasingly comes from meaningful unpaid activities. People can engage in exploration, self-improvement, volunteering or whatever else they find satisfying. Greater social engagement would be supported.

As an American who grew up believing in the virtues of traditional work, this last point intrigues me. I saw many people in the baby boomer generation stop paid work *early* in their 50s. Some have thrived; many have suffered.

Using these six tenets to guide our decisions as individuals and organizations, we can move toward a positive future. Some tenets can be accomplished on an individual level (move toward fulfilling jobs and civic empowerment). Other tenets operate at an organizational level (realigned companies and human-centric AI). The remaining tenets relate to a governmental level (shared economic prosperity and flexible labor markets).

How does this vision of the future make you feel? Excited? Scared? Happy? Worried?

SUMMARY

As AI assumes more traditional work, we can focus on being better humans at work. Having less work, we can give up our culture of busyness and focus more on meaning. We can make better human connections. We can be more in sync with one another. We can engage in more meaningful activities.

If you are like me, you plan to work for decades to come. I believe we owe it to the next generations to start making this change toward more humanism at work. The future has arrived, and small changes will add up quickly if we all step in and do our part.

I challenge you to tolerate the discomfort and embrace the future of work now. Let's disrupt the status quo. Let's make work not suck.

Acknowledgments

If you have made it this far, you are likely experiencing cognitive overload. Your brain might hurt.

Writing this book was a new, scary, exciting, and creative endeavor. I stepped out of my comfort zone to share personal stories. I challenged my own assumptions about work. I reexamined my own time management, communication, and empathy skills and found ways to improve. It wasn't easy, and it wasn't always fun.

I hope you understand more about the human brain and behavior and a lot more about the workplace. I hope you are inspired to shake things up at work and have a little fun.

Time is the most precious thing we have, and I sincerely appreciate your time and attention in reading my book.

Thank you.

A big thank you to my interviewees for sharing your stories:

Arin Fordstadt	Kate Snyder
Danielle Vaeth	Mike (anonymous)
Dave Joseph	Natasha VanWright
Dr. Ellen Walker	Nina Perales
Dr. Grace Terrell	Patrick Foley
Dr. Sabrina Starling	Randi Braun
Jacqueline Calamia	Richard Mathera
Jane (anonymous)	Sarah Dayes

Writing this book allowed me to reconnect with old friends and make new friends. I felt inspired by everyone who wants to make work not suck. Special thanks to all my sisters at CHIEF and my team at New Degree Press.

Thank you to everyone who preordered a copy of my book and donated to my prelaunch campaign:

Abby Donnelly	April Yearby
Abi Warren	Ashlea Johnson
Adele Welage	Ashley Herd
Alan Liebert	Ashley Jones Lee
Alex Kurland	Ashok Mathur
Allison Palombo	Ben Frauhiger
Alston Wang	Ben Grimes
Amy Horner, CPA, MBA	Beth Patino
Amy Warner	Beverly Wallace
Andrew McCoy	Boris Kaplunovsky
Andy Smitley	Brigid Schulte
Anjlee Joshi	Brigitte Specht
Anne Marie Watkins	Cameron Graham, MPH

Carlo Mahfouz
Carrie Nelson
Cecilia Edwards
Chantelle Schenning
Chappell Phillips
Chip Baggett
Chris Marshall
Christie Fleming
Christine Chandler
Colleen Runyon
Connie Hudnall
Dan Blackburn
Danielle Vaeth
Dave Joseph
David Guernsey
David Johnson
David Shinn
Debbi Miranda
Denise Stahl
Derrick Duplessy
Dionne Lewis
Dr. Alan Schlechter
Dr. Art Kelley
Dr. Balu Gadhe
Dr. Brian Hepburn
Dr. Cristine Oropez
Dr. David Eisenberg
Dr. Ellen Walker
Dr. Ethan Basch
Dr. Grace Terrell
Dr. Jan Lee Santos
Dr. Jane Trinh

Dr. Jennifer Rucci
Dr. Jess Levy
Dr. Joanna Kmiecik
Dr. Jose Gonzalez
Dr. Justin Hunt
Dr. Laura Halpin
Dr. Mark Russ
Dr. Mia McNeil
Dr. Michael Hochman
Dr. Miriam Zylberglait
Lisigurski
Dr. Nate Copeland
Dr. Nora Dennis
Dr. Nyota Pieh
Dr. Payam Parvinchiha
Dr. Prakash Masand
Dr. Rachel Keever
Dr. Ramon Jacobs-Shaw
Dr. Robert Trestman
Dr. Sandeep Palakodeti
Dr. Sandeep Patel
Dr. Scott Klenzak
Dr. Surah Grumet
Dr. Syed Sumair
Dr. Vinay Saranga
Dr. Yun Boylston
Dr. Zach Feldman
Eden Ezell
Ellen Johnson
Emily Hales
Eric Koester
Eric Martinson

Erica Lofving
Erik Barnett
Erin Keyes
Esther Howard
Geoffrey Jones
Georgia Mitchell
Gillian Cummings-Beck
Greg Pate
Gregory Davis
Hannah Austin
Igor Gorlatov
Ilya Tabakh
Jackie Beery
Jackie Choi
Jake Fox
James Lydiard
Jane Bers
Jasmine Ahmed
Jason Jenkins
Jenn Browning
Jennifer (Albertalli)
Kleinhenz
Jennifer L Williams
Jennifer L Williams
Jeremy Alexander
Jill Laing
Jill Pollander
Joanna Arencibia
Joe Pierangeli
Joel White
John Coyle
John Minahan

John Williford
John Williford
Jonathan Davis
Joseph Harrison
Julia Jezmir
K Grace Bell
Kamar Thomas
Kate Snyder
Kathleen Ross
Kathryn McCarthy
Katy Lanz
Keely Byrne
Kelly Cassaro
Kerri Brady
Kevin Berman
Kirsten Olshan
Kristie Altherr
Kristin Jamberdino
Kristina Natt och Dag
Lani Flores
Laura Cococcia
Laura Demuth
Laurea Salvatore
Lauren Feldman Hay
Laurie Canepa
Lawrence Andrusyszyn
Lee George
Leigh Burgess
Libby Batcha
Lisa DeAngelis
Lisa McCurdy
Lisa Shock

Liz Lax
Liz Weingast
Lizette Warner
Lucy Chen
Malinda Lowery
Margot Rosenstein
Marianne Bers
Mark Sampang
Mary McGuire
Matt Mayabb
Maura Charles
Meera Atkins
Meghan Pellerin
Melanie Varin
Michelle Ferguson
Michelle Manassah
Michelle Pecak
Mike Johnson
Mike Maley
Miriam Rosenau
Moisha Platto
Nadya Karyo
Natalia Roberts
Natasha Durkins
Natasha VanWright
Nina Perales
Nitu Sharma
Os (Osnat) Benari
Paige Nelson
Pamela Oberg
Patricia Parnell
Patrick Foley

Paula Doroff
Pauline Kabitsis
Penny Boyle
Rachael Jones
Rachel Eisenberg
Randi Braun
Randi Roy
Rhone D'Errico
Richard Mathera
Robin Caruso
Ronald Blanchard
Roshunda Harris-Allen
Rui Negrões Soares
Ryker Henriksen
Saima Siddiqui
Sami Horn
Sarah Dayes
Sarah Jacobson
Sarah Krepp
Sarah Pokorny
Scott White
Seth Staton
Shaun E Garcia
Shelly Ravenscraft
Shelly Twigg
Sloane Nichols
Soumya Padala
Stacy Olsen DiStefano
Stephanie Falkenstein
Stephanie Hillis
Stephanie Lemek
Stephen Eng

Stephen Keene
Steve Powell
Susan Foosness
Susan Whittemore
Suzanne Roske
Taylor Zublena
Tina Loarte-Rodriguez
Tom Byrne
Tom Gray
Tonya J Long
Tracy Dodd
Tracy Higgins
Tracy Kogan
Tracy Tillery
Urvashi Bhatnagar
Wayne Briggs
Wayne Maiorono
Wendy Bailey
Wendy Marshall
Wendy Stusrud
Xinjin Zhao
Zundra Bryant

Appendix

———

INTRODUCTION

Apollo Technical LLC. 2022. "Statistics on Remote Workers That
Will Surprise You (2022)." Apollo Technical LLC. https://www.
apollotechnical.com/statistics-on-remote-workers/.

Monster staff. 2020. "Yes, You Can Still Burn out-Even While
Working from Home." Monster Career Advice. https://www.
monster.com/career-advice/article/overworked.

Ozimek, Dr. Adam. 2021. "Economist Report: Future Workforce
| Upwork." Upwork. https://www.upwork.com/press/releases/
economist-report-future-workforce.

Parker, Kim, Juliana Menasce Horowitz, and Rachel Minkin. 2021.
"How the Coronavirus Outbreak Has—and Hasn't—Changed
the Way Americans Work." Pew Research Center's Social &
Demographic Trends Project. Pew Research Center. https://
www.pewresearch.org/social-trends/2020/12/09/how-the-coro-
navirus-outbreak-has-and-hasnt-changed-the-way-americans-
work/.

Ratan, Rabindra, Dave B. Miller, and Jeremy N. Bailenson. 2022. "Facial Appearance Dissatisfaction Explains Differences in Zoom Fatigue." *Cyberpsychology, Behavior, and Social Networking* 25, no. 2 (2022): 124–29. https://doi.org/10.1089/cyber.2021.0112.

Reynolds, Brie Weiler. 2021. "FlexJobs, Mental Health America Survey: Mental Health in the Workplace." FlexJobs Job Search Tips and Blog. FlexJobs.com. https://www.flexjobs.com/blog/post/flexjobs-mha-mental-health-workplace-pandemic/.

Schulte, Brigid. 2022. "The Case Against the Ideal Worker." BrigidSchulte.com. http://www.brigidschulte.com/resources/the-case-against-the-ideal-worker/.

Slack. 2020. "Report: Remote Work in the Age of Covid-19." Slack. https://slack.com/blog/collaboration/report-remote-work-during-coronavirus.

CHAPTER 1

Grant, Adam. 2021. "Mood of the Year: Languishing." Pocket. https://getpocket.com/collections/mood-of-the-year-languishing.

Kubrick, Stanley, director. 1980. *The Shining*. Warner Bros. 146 minutes.

Pajer, Nicole. 2021. "Adults Need Playtime as Much as Kids." Shondaland. https://www.shondaland.com/live/body/a36123122/adults-need-playtime-as-much-as-kids/.

Santos, Dr. Laurie. 2022. "Fighting That 'Meh' Feeling of Languishing: The Happiness Lab with Dr. Laurie Santos." Pushkin Industries. https://www.pushkin.fm/podcasts/the-happiness-lab-with-dr-laurie-santos/fighting-that-meh-feeling-of-languishing.

Siviy, Stephen M. 2016. "A Brain Motivated to Play: Insights into the Neurobiology of Playfulness." *Behaviour* 153, no. 6-7 (2016): 819–44. https://doi.org/10.1163/1568539x-00003349.

Staff of the Morning. 2021. "The Year's Most Read." *The New York Times.* https://www.nytimes.com/2021/12/29/briefing/most-read-stories-times-2021.html.

CHAPTER 2

Csikszentmihalyi, Mihaly. 2009. *Flow: The Psychology of Optimal Experience.* New York: Harper and Row.

Erlich, Pippa, and James Reed, directors. 2020. *My Octopus Teacher.* Netflix. 90 minutes.

Godfrey-Smith, Peter. 2021. *Metazoa: Animal Life and the Birth of the Mind.* New York: Picador.

Miller, Arthur I. 2002. *Einstein, Picasso: Space, Time and the Beauty That Causes Havoc.* New York: BasicBooks.

Montgomery, Sy. 2016. *Soul of an Octopus.* New York: Simon & Schuster Ltd.

Newport, Cal. 2016. *Deep Work: Rules for Focused Success in a Distracted World*. New York: Grand Central Publishing.

Octolab TV. n.d. "Octolab TV." YouTube video. Accessed September 25, 2022. https://www.youtube.com/channel/UCNo_xQ7N-vTr31naPAcjQWjg/videos.

Schulte, Brigid. 2015. *Overwhelmed: Work, Love, and Play When No One Has the Time*. London: Bloomsbury.

TED. 2008. "Mihaly Csikszentmihalyi: Flow, the Secret to Happiness." October 24, 2008. 18 minutes. https://youtu.be/fXIeFJC-qsPs.

Zadra, Antonio. 2022. *When Brains Dream: Exploring the Science and Mystery of Sleep*. New York: WW Norton.

CHAPTER 3

Brewer, Noel T., Jessica T. DeFrank, and Melissa B. Gilkey. 2016. "Anticipated Regret and Health Behavior: A Meta-Analysis." *Health Psychology* 35, no. 11 (2016): 1264–75. https://doi.org/10.1037/hea0000294.

Budnick, Christopher J., Arielle P. Rogers, and Larissa K. Barber. 2020. "The Fear of Missing out at Work: Examining Costs and Benefits to Employee Health and Motivation." *Computers in Human Behavior* 104 (2020): 106161. https://doi.org/10.1016/j.chb.2019.106161.

Coricelli, Giorgio, Hugo D Critchley, Mateus Joffily, John P O'Doherty, Angela Sirigu, and Raymond J Dolan. 2005. "Regret and Its Avoidance: A Neuroimaging Study of Choice Behavior." *Nature Neuroscience* 8, no. 9 (2005): 1255–62. https://doi.org/10.1038/nn1514.

Free to Focus. n.d. "Free to Focus." Accessed September 24, 2022. https://freetofocus.com/.

Gourley, S. L., K. S. Zimmermann, A. G. Allen, and J. R. Taylor. 2016. "The Medial Orbitofrontal Cortex Regulates Sensitivity to Outcome Value." *Journal of Neuroscience* 36, no. 16 (2016): 4600–4613. https://doi.org/10.1523/jneurosci.4253-15.2016.

Hobson, Nick. 2018. "The Science of FOMO and What We're Really Missing out On." *Psychology Today.* April 23, 2018. https://www.psychologytoday.com/us/blog/ritual-and-the-brain/201804/the-science-fomo-and-what-we-re-really-missing-out.

Irrational Labs. n.d. "Behaviorally Informed Design for Better Products and a Better World." Irrational Labs. Accessed September 20, 2022. https://irrationallabs.com/.

Manson, Mark. 2016. *The Subtle Art of Not Giving a Fuck: A Counterintuitive Approach to Living a Good Life.* New York: HarperOne.

Mcleod, Saul. 1970. "Social Roles." Simply Psychology. https://www.simplypsychology.org/social-roles.html#:~:text=Social%20norms%20are%20the%20unwritten,order%20and%20predictability%20in%20society.

The Decision Lab. n.d. "Regret Aversion." The Decision Lab. Accessed September 24, 2022. https://thedecisionlab.com/biases/regret-aversion.

Seiler, Michael, Vicky Seiler, Stefan Traub, and David Harrison. 2008. "Regret Aversion and False Reference Points in Residential Real Estate." *Journal of Real Estate Research* 30, no. 4 (2008): 461–74. https://doi.org/10.1080/10835547.2008.12091229.

Şentürk, Erman, Eser Sağaltıcı, Bahadır Geniş, and Ömür Günday Toker. 2021. "Predictors of Depression, Anxiety and Stress among Remote Workers during the COVID-19 Pandemic." *Work* 70, no. 1 (2021): 41–51. https://doi.org/10.3233/wor-210082.

Sugihto, Esther. 2016. "The Law of Propinquity." Medium. https://medium.com/@social_archi/the-law-of-propinquity-f16502b6c842.

Varma, Prerna, Moira Junge, Hailey Meaklim, and Melinda L. Jackson. 2021. "Younger People Are More Vulnerable to Stress, Anxiety and Depression during COVID-19 Pandemic: A Global Cross-Sectional Survey." *Progress in Neuro-Psychopharmacology and Biological Psychiatry* 109 (2021): 110236. https://doi.org/10.1016/j.pnpbp.2020.110236.

CHAPTER 4

Berkun, Scott. 2021. "The Cult of Busy." ScottBerkun.com https://scottberkun.com/2010/the-cult-of-busy/.

Brewer, Judson A., Patrick D. Worhunsky, Jeremy R. Gray, Yi-Yuan Tang, Jochen Weber, and Hedy Kober. 2011. "Meditation Experience Is Associated with Differences in Default Mode Network Activity and Connectivity." *Proceedings of the National Academy of Sciences* 108, no. 50 (2011): 20254–59. https://doi.org/10.1073/pnas.1112029108.

Miro. n.d. "Distributed 2021 Day 1 Recordings and Resources | Miro." Accessed September 25, 2022. https://community.miro.com/events-44/distributed-2021-day-1-recordings-and-resources-6288.

Miro. n.d. "The Visual Collaboration Platform for Every Team: Miro." Miro. Accessed September 25, 2022. http://www.miro.com/.

Fitzgerald, F. Scott. 1925. *The Great Gatsby.* New York: Charles Scribner's Sons.

Fontinelle, Amy. 2022. "A Brief History of Taxes in the US" Investopedia. https://www.investopedia.com/articles/tax/10/history-taxes.asp.

Hamermesh, Daniel S, and Jungmin Lee. 2007. "Stressed out on Four Continents: Time Crunch or Yuppie Kvetch?" *Review of Economics and Statistics* 89, no. 2 (2007): 374–83. https://doi.org/10.1162/rest.89.2.374.

Imtiaz, Ayesha. 2021. "The Way We View Free Time Is Making Us Less Happy." BBC Worklife. https://www.bbc.com/worklife/article/20210914-the-way-we-view-free-time-is-making-us-less-happy.

Jabr, Ferris. 2013. "Why Your Brain Needs More Downtime." *Scientific American*. https://www.scientificamerican.com/article/mental-downtime/.

Love, Shayla. 2021. "Covid Changed Our Relationship to Busyness. Can We Keep It That Way?" VICE. https://www.vice.com/en/article/k78wpz/covid-changed-our-relationship-to-busyness-can-we-keep-it-that-way-v28n2.

Muti, Francesco. 2007. "The Strange, Modern Cult of Being Busy." *Toronto Star*. https://www.thestar.com/news/insight/2007/08/10/the_strange_modern_cult_of_being_busy.html.

New America. n.d. "Better Life Lab." New America. Accessed September 25, 2022. https://www.newamerica.org/better-life-lab/.

Schulte, Brigid. 2015. *Overwhelmed: Work, Love, and Play When No One Has the Time*. London: Bloomsbury, 2015.

Schulte, Brigid. 2014. "Why Being Too Busy Makes Us Feel So Good." *The Washington Post*. https://www.washingtonpost.com/opinions/why-being-too-busy-makes-us-feel-so-good/2014/03/14/c098f6c8-9e81-11e3-a050-dc3322a94fa7_story.html.

The Library of Congress. n.d. "America at Leisure: Articles and Essays: America at Work, America at Leisure: Motion Pictures from 1894-1915." Digital Collections: Library of Congress. The Library of Congress. Accessed September 25, 2022.

https://www.loc.gov/collections/america-at-work-and-leisure-1894-to-1915/articles-and-essays/america-at-leisure/.

Veblen, Thorstein. 1961. *The Theory of the Leisure Class: An Economic Study of Institutions; with a Foreword by Stuart Chase.* New York: Random House.

CHAPTER 5

Bellis, Mary. 2019. "Who Invented Emoticons and Emoji?" ThoughtCo. https://www.thoughtco.com/emoticons-and-emoji-1991412#:~:text=Professor%20Scott%20Fahlman%2C%20a%20computer,was%20a%20smiley%20face%20%3A%2D).

Blumenthal, Amy. 2015. "Why Haven't They Replied Yet?" USC. https://viterbi.usc.edu/news/news/2015/why-hasn-t.htm.

Ceci, L. 2022. "Emails Sent per Day 2025." Statista. https://www.statista.com/statistics/456500/daily-number-of-emails-worldwide/.

Churches, Owen, Mike Nicholls, Myra Thiessen, Mark Kohler, and Hannah Keage. 2014. "Emoticons in Mind: An Event-Related Potential Study." *Social Neuroscience* 9, no. 2 (2014): 196–202. https://doi.org/10.1080/17470919.2013.873737.

Coursera, n.d. "Wonders of Ancient Egypt." Coursera. Accessed September 25, 2022. https://www.coursera.org/learn/wonders-ancient-egypt.

Dhawan, Erica. 2021. *Digital Body Language*. London: Harper-Collins Publishers.

The Guardian. 2016. "How Did Email Grow from Messages between Academics to a Global Epidemic?" Guardian News and Media. https://www.theguardian.com/technology/2016/mar/07/email-ray-tomlinson-history.

Matsumoto, David, and Hyi Sung Hwang. 2011. "Reading Facial Expressions of Emotion." American Psychological Association. https://www.apa.org/science/about/psa/2011/05/facial-expressions.

Parker, Kim, and Juliana Menasce Horowitz. 2022. "Majority of Workers Who Quit a Job in 2021 Cite Low Pay, No Opportunities for Advancement, Feeling Disrespected." Pew Research Center. https://www.pewresearch.org/fact-tank/2022/03/09/majority-of-workers-who-quit-a-job-in-2021-cite-low-pay-no-opportunities-for-advancement-feeling-disrespected/.

Slack. n.d. "Slack Is Your Digital HQ." Slack. Accessed September 25, 2022. https://slack.com/.

The Penn Museum. n.d. "Home—Penn Museum." Accessed September 25, 2022. https://www.penn.museum/.

The University of Pennsylvania. n.d. "The University of Pennsylvania." University of Pennsylvania. Accessed September 25, 2022. https://www.upenn.edu/.

Wise, Jason. 2022. "How Many Emails Does the Average Person Receive per Day in 2022?" EarthWeb. https://

earthweb.com/how-many-emails-does-the-average-person-re-ceive-per-day/#:~:text=According%20to%20email%20receiv-ing%20statistics,Yes%2C%20that%20is%20a%20lot!

CHAPTER 6

Bailenson, Jeremy N. 2021. "Nonverbal Overload: A Theoretical Argument for the Causes of Zoom Fatigue." *Technology, Mind, and Behavior* 2, no. 1 (2021). https://doi.org/10.1037/tmb0000030.

Booker, Christopher. 2019. *Seven Basic Plots: Why We Tell Stories.* London: Bloomsbury Continuum.

Creator Institute. n.d. "Book Creators: Write Better, Write Together." Creator Institute. Accessed September 25, 2022. https://www.creator.institute/.

Eber, Karen. n.d. "How Your Brain Responds to Stories — and Why They're Crucial for Leaders." TEDx Talk. Accessed September 25, 2022. https://www.ted.com/talks/karen_eber_how_your_brain_responds_to_stories_and_why_they_re_crucial_for_leaders/transcript?language=en.

Heath, Chip, and Heath, Dan. 2010. *Switch: How to Change Things When Change Is Hard.* New York: Crown Business.

Jachimowica, Jon M., Shannon Duncan, Weber, Elke U., and John-son, Eric. 2019. "When and Why Defaults Influence Decisions: A Meta-Analysis of Default Effects." *Behavioural Public Policy* 3, no. 02 (2019): 159–86. https://doi.org/10.1017/bpp.2018.43.

Vanguard. 2021. "Automatic enrollment: The power of the default." Vanguard. https://institutional.vanguard.com/iam/pdf/ISGAE_022020.pdf.

VHIL. n.d. "Zoom Exhaustion & Fatigue Scale." VHIL. Accessed September 25, 2022. https://www.stanfordvr.com/pubs/2021/zoom-exhaustion-fatigue-scale/.

CHAPTER 7

Anderson, David, and Rebecca Wilkin. 2021. "What Staring at a Screen All Day Does to Your Brain and Body." *Business Insider*. https://www.businessinsider.com/screen-time-effects-health-vision-staring-at-screens-bad-for-you-2019-1.

BBC. 2010. "The Rubber Hand Illusion—Horizon: Is Seeing Believing?—BBC Two." YouTube video. 3 minutes. https://www.youtube.com/watch?v=sxwn1w7MJvk&feature=youtu.be.

Chen, Connie, and Amir Ismael. 2022. "The 12 Best Places to Buy Blue-Light Blocking Computer Glasses, Whether You Need Prescription Lenses or Not." *Insider*. https://www.insider.com/guides/style/blue-light-computer-glasses-brands.

Cuddy, Amy. n.d. "Your Body Language May Shape Who You Are." TEDx Talk. Accessed September 25, 2022. https://www.ted.com/talks/amy_cuddy_your_body_language_may_shape_who_you_are?language=en.

Montgomery, Sy. 2016. *Soul of an Octopus*. New York: Simon & Schuster Ltd.

Naftulin, Julia. 2019. "A New Study Suggests Screen Time Could Delay Children's Communication, Motor, and Problem-Solving Skills." *Business Insider.* https://www.businessinsider.com/screen-time-could-delay-child-development-study-2019-1.

Newport, Cal. 2021. "Can Virtual Reality Fix the Workplace?" *The New Yorker.* https://www.newyorker.com/culture/office-space/can-virtual-reality-fix-the-workplace.

Newport, Cal. 2016. *Deep Work: Rules for Focused Success in a Distracted World.* New York: Grand Central Publishing.

Putka, Sophie. 2021. "What Is Blue Light? How It Affects Your Health, Ways You Can Control Your Exposure, and When to Use Blue Light Glasses." *Business Insider.* https://www.businessinsider.com/guides/tech/what-is-blue-light.

Rohde, Marieke, Massimiliano Di Luca, and Marc O. Ernst. 2011. "The Rubber Hand Illusion: Feeling of Ownership and Proprioceptive Drift Do Not Go Hand in Hand." *PLoS ONE* 6, no. 6 (2011). https://doi.org/10.1371/journal.pone.0021659.

Tangermann, Victor. 2018. "I Tried Apple's Screen Time Tool and Was Shocked by the Amount of Time I Actually Spend on My Phone." *Business Insider.* https://www.businessinsider.com/apple-screen-time-tool-increased-time-spend-phone-2018-8.

University of Washington. n.d. "Brain facts and figures." University of Washington. Accessed September 25, 2022. https://faculty.washington.edu/chudler/facts.html.

CHAPTER 8

Atwater, Eastwood. 1981. *I Hear You: Listening Skills to Make You a Better Manager.* Englewood Cliffs, NJ: Prentice-Hall.

Brady, Timothy F., Viola S. Störmer, and George A. Alvarez. 2016. "Working Memory Is Not Fixed-Capacity: More Active Storage Capacity for Real-World Objects than for Simple Stimuli." *Proceedings of the National Academy of Sciences* 113, no. 27 (2016): 7459–64. https://doi.org/10.1073/pnas.1520027113.

Chai, Wen Jia, Aini Ismafairus Abd Hamid, and Jafri Malin Abdullah. 2018. "Working Memory from the Psychological and Neurosciences Perspectives: A Review." *Frontiers in Psychology* 9 (2018). https://doi.org/10.3389/fpsyg.2018.00401.

Freed, Joseph. 2020. "Council Post: Why Cognitive Load Could Be the Most Important Employee Experience Metric in the Next 10 Years." *Forbes Magazine.* https://www.forbes.com/sites/forbesbusinessdevelopmentcouncil/2020/06/30/why-cognitive-load-could-be-the-most-important-employee-experience-metric-in-the-next-10-years/?sh=3bd5e10b362f.

Funahashi, Shintaro. 2017. "Working Memory in the Prefrontal Cortex." *Brain Sciences* 7, no. 12 (2017): 49. https://doi.org/10.3390/brainsci7050049.

Hemp, Paul. 2014. "Death by Information Overload." *Harvard Business Review.* https://hbr.org/2009/09/death-by-information-overload.

Lackie, Bruce. 1977. "Nonverbal Communication in Clinical Social Work Practice." *Clinical Social Work Journal* 5, no. 1 (1977): 43–52. https://doi.org/10.1007/bf02143599.

Levitt, Dana Heller. 2002. "Active Listening and Counselor Self-Efficacy." *The Clinical Supervisor* 20, no. 2 (2002): 101–15. https://doi.org/10.1300/j001v20n02_09.

Lovell, Oliver. 2020 *Sweller's Cognitive Load Theory in Action*. Melton, Woodbridge: John Catt Educational Ltd.

Maley, Claude H. 2012. *Project Management Concepts, Methods, and Techniques*. Boca Raton, FL: CRC Press.

Miriam-Webster Dictionary. "Miriam-Webster Dictionary." Miriam-Webster. Accessed September 25, 2022. https://www.merriam-webster.com/dictionary.

Newman, Ruth G., Marie A. Danziger, and Mark Cohen. 1987. *Communicating in Business Today*. Lexington, MA: D.C. Heath.

Singh Ospina, Naykky, Kari A. Phillips, Rene Rodriguez-Gutierrez, Ana Castaneda-Guarderas, Michael R. Gionfriddo, Megan E. Branda, and Victor M. Montori. 2018. "Eliciting the Patient's Agenda—Secondary Analysis of Recorded Clinical Encounters." *Journal of General Internal Medicine* 34, no. 1 (2018): 36–40. https://doi.org/10.1007/s11606-018-4540-5.

UTPB. 2020. "How Much of Communication Is Nonverbal?: UT Permian Basin Online." UTPB. https://online.utpb.edu/

about-us/articles/communication/how-much-of-communi-cation-is-nonverbal/.

CHAPTER 9

Academy of Family Physicians (AAFP). 2020. "Implicit Bias Resources." AAFP. https://www.aafp.org/family-physician/patient-care/the-everyone-project/toolkit/implicit-bias.html.

Barrett, Paul, Justin Hendrix, and Grant Sims. 2022. "How Tech Platforms Fuel US Political Polarization and What Government Can Do about It." Brookings. https://www.brookings.edu/blog/techtank/2021/09/27/how-tech-platforms-fuel-u-s-political-polarization-and-what-government-can-do-about-it/.

Gladwell, Malcolm. 2005. *Blink: The Power of Thinking Without Thinking*. London: Penguin Books.

Hao, Karen. 2022. "The Coming War on the Hidden Algorithms That Trap People in Poverty." *MIT Technology Review*. https://www.technologyreview.com/2020/12/04/1013068/algorithms-create-a-poverty-trap-lawyers-fight-back/.

Mergenthaler, Philipp, Ute Lindauer, Gerald A. Dienel, and Andreas Meisel. 2013. "Sugar for the Brain: The Role of Glucose in Physiological and Pathological Brain Function." *Trends in Neurosciences* 36, no. 10 (2013): 587–97. https://doi.org/10.1016/j.tins.2013.07.001.

Naskar, Abhijit, 2021. *The Shape of a Human: Our America, Their America*. Independent Publication.

Project Implicit. n.d. "Take a Test." Accessed September 25, 2022. https://implicit.harvard.edu/implicit/takeatest.html.

Schulte, Julius. 2019. "Ai-Assisted Recruitment Is Biased. Here's How to Make It More Fair." World Economic Forum. https://www.weforum.org/agenda/2019/05/ai-assisted-recruitment-is-biased-heres-how-to-beat-it/.

Sleek, Scott. 2018. "The Bias Beneath: Two Decades of Measuring Implicit Associations." Association for Psychological Science. https://www.psychologicalscience.org/observer/the-bias-beneath-two-decades-of-measuring-implicit-associations.

CHAPTER 10

Daniels, Greg, director. 2005. *The Office*. NBC.

English, Larry. 2021. *Office Optional: How to Build a Connected Culture with Virtual Teams*. Nakskov: Nota.

Gervais, Ricky, and Stephen Merchant, directors. 2001. *The Office*. BBC.

Insights. n.d. "Global Leader in Learning and Development Solutions." Insights. Accessed September 25, 2022. https://www.insights.com/us/.

James, Olivia, Paul Delfabbro, and Daniel L. King. 2021. "A Comparison of Psychological and Work Outcomes in Open-Plan and Cellular Office Designs: A Systematic Review." *SAGE Open* 11, no. 1 (2021): 215824402098886. https://doi.org/10.1177/2158244020988869.

Judge, Mike, director. 1999. *Office Space*. Judgemental Films. 89 minutes.

Miro. n.d. "The Visual Collaboration Platform for Every Team: Miro." Miro. Accessed September 25, 2022. http://www.miro.com/.

Rattner, Donald M. 2019. "Why Your Conference Room Table Is Probably Bad for Business." *Work Design Magazine*. https://www.workdesign.com/2019/03/why-your-conference-room-table-is-probably-bad-for-business/.

Slack. n.d. "Slack Is Your Digital HQ." Slack. Accessed September 25, 2022. https://slack.com/.

Tirado, Bernardo. 2012. "The Power Seat: Where You Sit Matters." *Psychology Today*. https://www.psychologytoday.com/us/blog/digital-leaders/201210/the-power-seat-where-you-sit-matters.

Tulshyan, Ruchika. 2021. "Return to Office? Some Women of Color Aren't Ready." *The New York Times*. https://www.nytimes.com/2021/06/23/us/return-to-office-anxiety.html.

CHAPTER 11

Armstrong, Kim. 2017. "'I Feel Your Pain:' The Neuroscience of Empathy." Association for Psychological Science. https://www.psychologicalscience.org/observer/neuroscience-empathy.

Cleveland Clinic. 2021. "Empathy Fatigue: How It Takes a Toll on You." Cleveland Clinic. https://health.clevelandclinic.org/

empathy-fatigue-how-stress-and-trauma-can-take-a-toll-on-you/.

C-Span. 1992. "User Clip: Clinton's I Feel Your Pain Moment." C-Span. https://www.c-span.org/video/?c4842764%2Fuser-clip-clintons-feel-pain-moment.

Fernández-Aráoz, Claudio. 2014. "Ignore Emotional Intelligence at Your Own Risk." *Harvard Business Review.* https://hbr. org/2014/10/ignore-emotional-intelligence-at-you-own-risk.

Herrera, Fernanda, Jeremy Bailenson, Erika Weisz, Elise Ogle, and Jamil Zaki. 2018. "Building Long-Term Empathy: A Large-Scale Comparison of Traditional and Virtual Reality Perspective-Taking." *PLOS ONE* 13, no. 10 (2018). https://doi. org/10.1371/journal.pone.0204494.

Hunnes, Dana Ellis. 2017. "Non-Human Animals Show Empathy. What Happened to Ours?" *HuffPost.* https://www.huffpost. com/entry/nonhuman-animals-show-emp_b_10949070#:~:- text=However%2C%20we%20now%20know%20that,a%20 wide%20range%20of%20emotions.

Montemayor, Carlos, Jodi Halpern, and Abrol Fairweather. 2021. "In Principle Obstacles for Empathic AI: Why We Can't Replace Human Empathy in Healthcare." *AI & SOCIETY.* https://doi. org/10.1007/s00146-021-01230-z.

Paiva, Andre. 2022. "Empathy for Autism with Virtual Reality." ClassVR. https://www.classvr.com/blog/empathy-for-au- tism-with-virtual-reality/#:~:text=Empathy%20for%20Oth- ers,can%20lead%20to%20certain%20behaviours.

Rutkin, Aviva Hope. 2013. "Inside the Mind of a Killer Whale: A Q+A with the Neuroscientist from 'Blackfish.'" The Raptor Lab. https://theraptorlab.wordpress.com/2013/08/14/inside-the-mind-of-a-killer-whale-a-qa-with-the-neuroscientist-from-blackfish/.

Singal, Vinamrata. 2021. "Mini-Sabbaticals: An Antidote to Burnout." Medium. https://medium.com/@vinamratasingal/mini-sabbaticals-an-antidote-to-burnout-60474dc18950#:~:-text=Longer%20explanation%3A%20A%20mini%20sabbati-cal,get%20out%20of%20my%20time.

SSNL. n.d. "Stanford Research." SSNL. Accessed September 25, 2022. https://www.ssnl.stanford.edu/research.

CHAPTER 12

Bariso, Justin. 2018. "There Are Actually 3 Types of Empathy. Here's How They Differ—and How You Can Develop Them All." Inc.com. https://www.inc.com/justin-bariso/there-are-actually-3-types-of-empathy-heres-how-they-differ-and-how-you-can-develop-them-all.html.

David, Jacques Louis. 1787. The Death of Socrates. New York. The Met.

Human Resources Degrees. n.d. "What Is the History of Human Resources?" Human Resources Degrees. Accessed July 14, 2022. https://www.humanresourcesmba.net/faq/what-is-the-history-of-human-resources/.

Konrath, Sara H., Edward H. O'Brien, and Courtney Hsing. 2010. "Changes in Dispositional Empathy in American College Students over Time: A Meta-Analysis." *Personality and Social Psychology Review* 15, no. 2 (2010): 180–98. https://doi.org/10.1177/1088868310377395.

Mackes, Nuria K., Dennis Golm, Owen G. O'Daly, Sagari Sarkar, Edmund J.S. Sonuga-Barke, Graeme Fairchild, and Mitul A. Mehta. 2018. "Tracking Emotions in the Brain—Revisiting the Empathic Accuracy Task." *NeuroImage* 178 (2018): 677–86. https://doi.org/10.1016/j.neuroimage.2018.05.080.

Marr, Bernard. 2018. "Why We No Longer Need HR Departments." LinkedIn. https://www.linkedin.com/pulse/20131118060732-64875646-why-we-no-longer-need-hr-departments/.

Nasher Museum. n.d. "Nasher Museum of Art at Duke University." Accessed September 23, 2022. https://nasher.duke.edu/.

Rothko, Mark. 1958. *No. 16 (Red, Brown, and Black)*. New York. MOMA.

Taylor, Derrick Bryson. 2020. "George Floyd Protests: A Timeline." *The New York Times.* https://www.nytimes.com/article/george-floyd-protests-timeline.html.

Thomas, Hank Willis. 2015. *Ain't Gonna Let Nobody Turn Us Around*. Durham, NC. The Nasher.

CHAPTER 13

Azor, Adriana. 2020. "What Happens to Your Brain When You Try to Multitask." Medium. https://medium.com/brainchronicles/what-happens-to-your-brain-when-you-try-to-multitask-ad699fe66500.

Conference2Go. n.d. "10 Excellent Reasons to Attend Academic Conferences." Conference2Go, Accessed August 20, 2022. https://www.conference2go.com/blog/reasons-to-attend-academic-conferences/.

Council, Young Entrepreneur. 2016. "Council Post: Four Critical Elements of a Successful Company Retreat." *Forbes.* https://www.forbes.com/sites/theyec/2016/08/12/four-critical-elements-of-a-successful-company-retreat/?sh=3fcc54cf767a.

Farnam Street. 2020. "Regression toward the Mean: An Introduction with Examples." Farnam Street. https://fs.blog/regression-to-the-mean/#:~:text=The%20notion%20of%20regression%20to,followed%20by%20more%20moderate%20ones.

Gewin, Virginia. 2019. "How the Scientific Meeting Has Changed since Nature's Founding 150 Years Ago." Nature News. Nature Publishing Group. December 18, 2019. https://www.nature.com/articles/d41586-019-03851-3.

MacKay, Jory. 2021. "Context Switching: Why Jumping between Tasks Is Killing Your Productivity." RescueTime Blog. February 9, 2021. https://blog.rescuetime.com/context-switching/#:~:text=According%20to%20psychologist%20Gerald%20Weinberg,of%20your%20productive%20time%20available.

Newport, Cal. 2016. *Deep Work: Rules for Focused Success in a Distracted World: Rules for Focused Success in a Distracted World*. New York: Grand Central Publishing.

Pham, Thanh. 2021. "The 'Touch It Once' Principle That Will Skyrocket Your Personal Efficiency." Asian Efficiency. https://www.asianefficiency.com/mindsets/touch-it-once-productivity-principle/.

Starling, Sabrina. 2021. *The Four Week Vacation*. Independently Published.

CHAPTER 14

Byrne, Jennie. 2013. "Conflict Resolution in 6 Simple Easy Steps." YouTube video. 14 minutes. https://www.youtube.com/watch?v=DSGy5yvCohM.

Kilmann. 2020. "Take the Thomas-Kilmann Conflict Mode Instrument (TKI) Take This Assessment Tool and Discover Which of the Five Conflict Modes You Might Be Using Too Much or Too Little... or Just Right." Kilmann Diagnostics. https://kilmanndiagnostics.com/overview-thomas-kilmann-conflict-mode-instrument-tki/.

Scott, Kim. 2019. *Radical Candor: Be a Kick-Ass Boss without Losing Your Humanity*. New York: St. Martin's Press.

Staben. n.d. "Staben: The Six-Step Conflict Resolution Process—Microsoft." WordPress Storage. Accessed September 25, 2022. https://wordpressstorageaccount.blob.core.windows.net/

wp-media/wp-content/uploads/sites/679/2018/07/Conflict-Resolution-Process-Resolution-Wkst.pdf.

CHAPTER 15

Nooyi, Indra. 2021. "Worklife with Adam Grant: Indra Nooyi Wants Us to Reimagine the Return to Work on Apple Podcasts." Interviewed by Adam Grant. Apple Podcasts. https://podcasts.apple.com/us/podcast/taken-for-granted-indra-nooyi-wants-us-to-reimagine/id1346314086?i=1000539774996.

McKinney, Scott Mayer, Marcin Sieniek, Varun Godbole, Jonathan Godwin, Natasha Antropova, Hutan Ashrafian, Trevor Back, et al. 2020. "International Evaluation of an AI System for Breast Cancer Screening." *Nature* 577, no. 7788 (2020): 89–94. https://doi.org/10.1038/s41586-019-1799-6.

Penttila, Nicky. 2019. "In Sync: How Humans Are Hard-Wired for Social Relationships." Dana Foundation. Dana Foundation. https://dana.org/article/in-sync-how-humans-are-hard-wired-for-social-relationships/.

Russell, Stuart, and Susskind, Daniel. 2021. "6 Positive AI Visions for the Future of Work." World Economic Forum. https://www.weforum.org/agenda/2021/11/positive-artificial-intelligence-visions-for-the-future-of-work/.

Susskind, Daniel. 2020. *A World Without Work*. New York: Metropolitan Books.

Uber Pro. n.d. "Driver Rewards with Uber Pro | Uber." Uber Pro. Accessed September 25, 2022. https://www.uber.com/hu/en/drive/uber-pro/.

Made in the USA
Monee, IL
21 January 2024